Discover
Britain's
historic
houses

The Midlands

Discover **Britain's**

Published by Reader's Digest Association Ltd
London • New York • Sydney • Montreal

historic houses
The Midlands

Simon Jenkins

Contents

2 LINCOLNSHIRE

4 NOTTINGHAMSHIRE

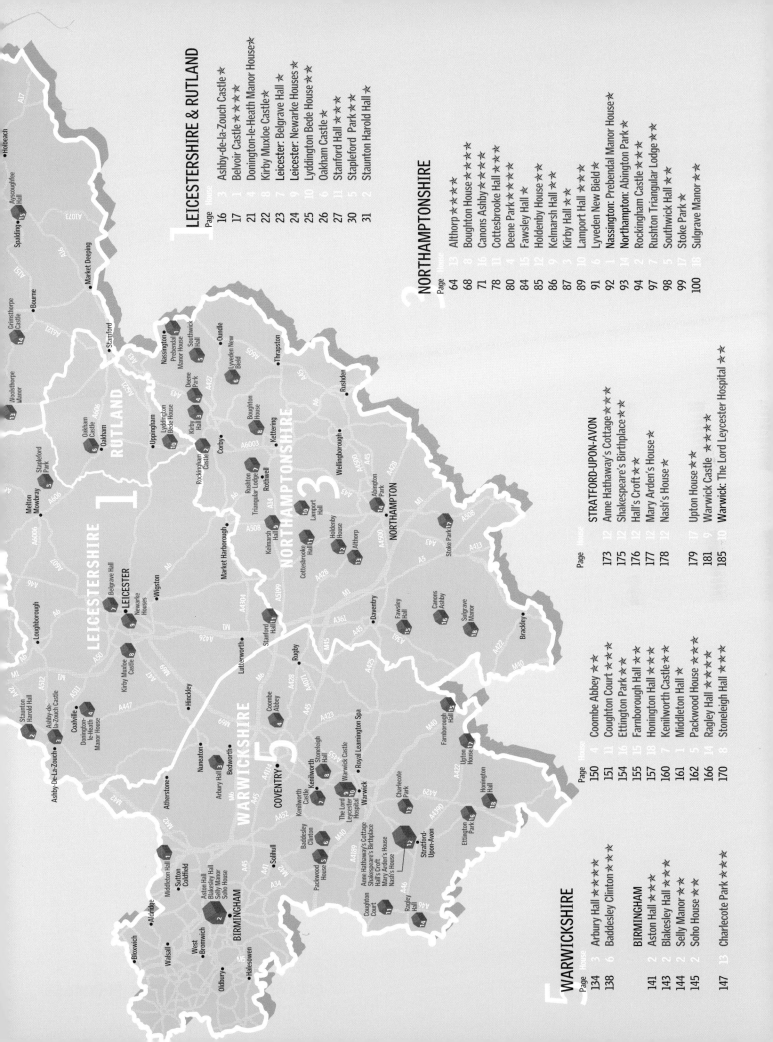

1 LEICESTERSHIRE & RUTLAND

NORTHAMPTONSHIRE

5 WARWICKSHIRE

BIRMINGHAM

STRATFORD-UPON-AVON

The best in Britain

SCOTLAND

- 114 Abbotsford, Melrose
- 127 Blair Castle
- 130 Cawdor Castle
- 128 Craigievar Castle
- 112 Drumlanrig Castle
- 131 Dunrobin Castle
- 129 Dunvegan Castle

- 126 Glamis Castle
- 120 Hill House
- 121 Hopetoun House
- 124 Inveraray Castle
- 117 Manderston
- 115 Mellerstain
- 118 Mount Stuart
- 119 New Lanark
- 122 Palace of Holyroodhouse
- 125 Scone Palace
- 132 Skara Brae
- 123 Stirling Castle
- 116 Thirlestane Castle
- 113 Traquair House

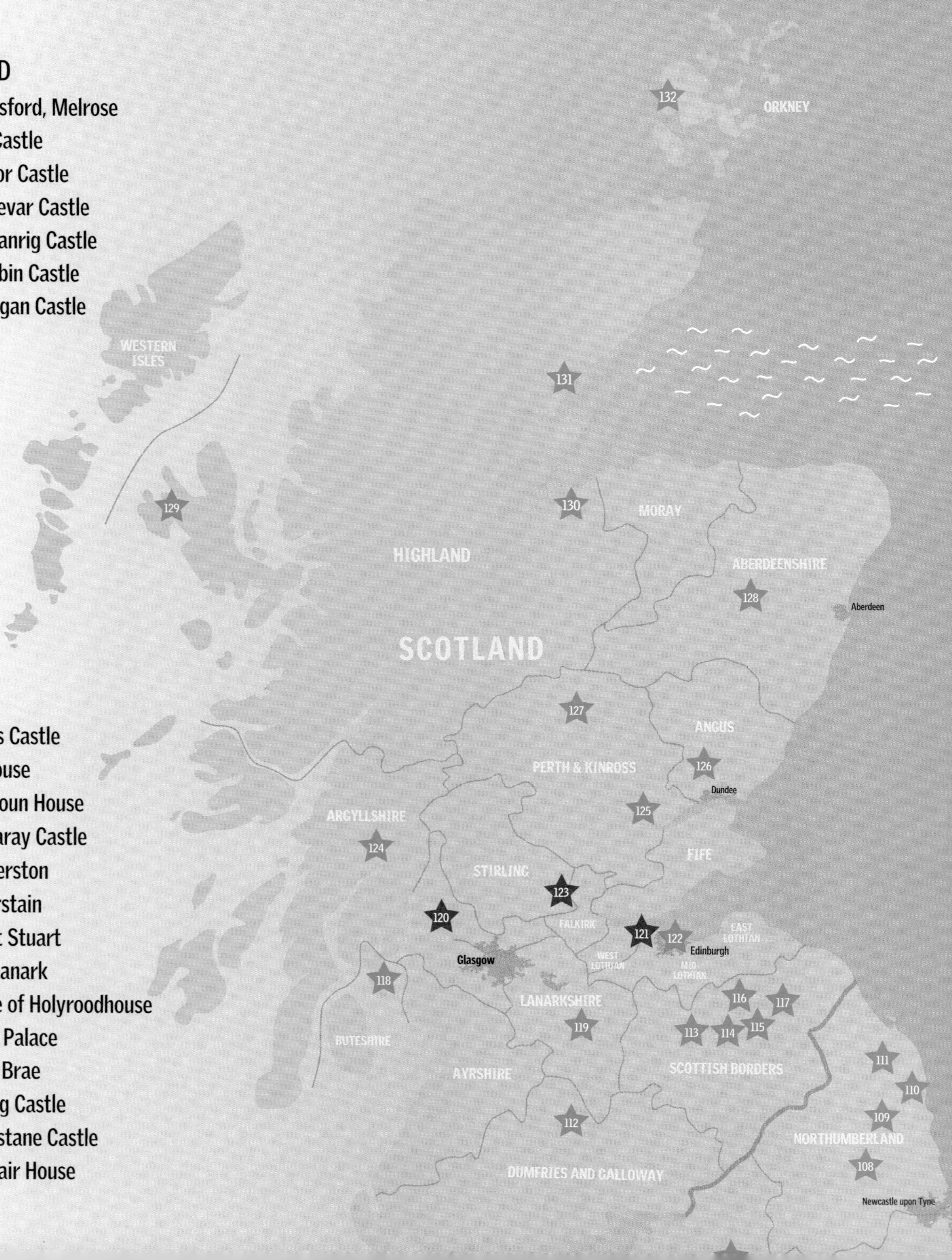
ORKNEY
WESTERN ISLES
HIGHLAND
SCOTLAND
MORAY
ABERDEENSHIRE
Aberdeen
ANGUS
Dundee
PERTH & KINROSS
ARGYLLSHIRE
STIRLING
FIFE
FALKIRK
WEST LOTHIAN
EAST LOTHIAN
MID-LOTHIAN
Edinburgh
Glasgow
LANARKSHIRE
BUTESHIRE
AYRSHIRE
SCOTTISH BORDERS
DUMFRIES AND GALLOWAY
NORTHUMBERLAND
Newcastle upon Tyne
Sunderland
132
131
129
130
128
127
126
125
124
123
120
121
122
118
119
116
117
113
114
115
112
111
110
109
108

- 61 Canons Ashby *
- 102 Castle Howard
- 14 Charleston
- 54 Chastleton
- 91 Chatsworth House
- 111 Chillingham Castle
- 36 Chiswick House
- 56 Claydon House
- 16 Cothay Manor
- 109 Cragside
- 70 Deene Park *
- 38 Dennis Severs House
- 28 Dyrham Park
- 52 Eastnor Castle
- 40 Eltham Palace
- 100 Fairfax House
- 13 Firle Place
- 3 Forde Abbey
- 27 Godinton Park
- 8 Goodwood House
- 78 Grimsthorpe Castle *
- 90 Haddon Hall
- 66 Hagley Hall
- 35 Ham House
- 34 Hampton Court
- 93 Hardwick Hall *
- 98 Harewood House
- 76 Harlaxton Manor *
- 65 Harvington Hall
- 51 Hatfield House

- 22 Hever Castle
- 80 Holkham Hall
- 37 Home House
- 79 Houghton Hall
- 107 Hutton-in-the-Forest
- 25 Ightham Mote
- 74 Kedleston Hall
- 21 Kensington Palace
- 5 Kingston Lacy
- 50 Knebworth House
- 24 Knole
- 29 Lacock Abbey
- 1 Lanhydrock
- 26 Leeds Castle
- 104 Levens Hall
- 19 Longleat
- 89 Lyme Park
- 53 Madresfield Court
- 48 Magdalen College
- 17 Montacute House
- 101 Newby Hall
- 94 Newstead Abbey *
- 96 Nostell Priory
- 6 Osborne House
- 32 Osterley Park
- 72 Oxburgh Hall
- 10 Parham House
- 23 Penshurst Place
- 9 Petworth House
- 106 Raby Castle
- 59 Ragley Hall *
- 41 Restoration House

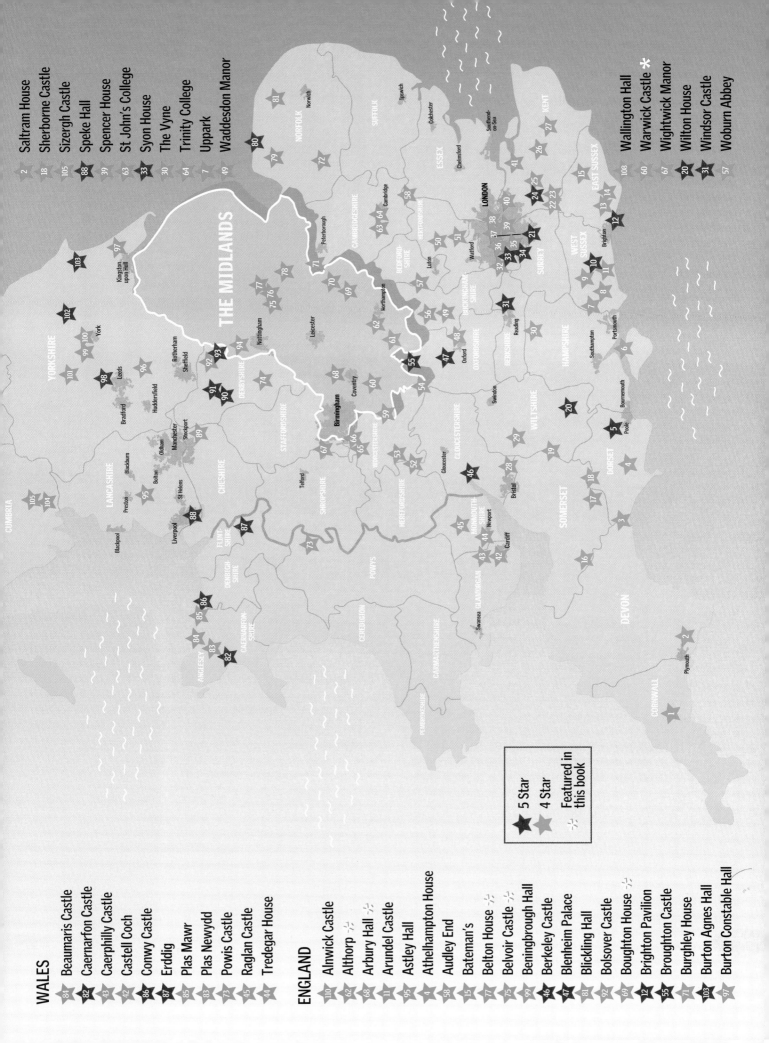

5 Star
4 Star
Featured in this book

WALES

ENGLAND

I visited these buildings after writing a book on English churches and the experience was as moving as it was different. While places of worship were built according to the authority and liturgy of the Church, people built houses for themselves. A house was useful first and beautiful second, and from this derives the joy of visiting houses. They are a conversation between utility and beauty down the ages.

In defining the word 'house' I soon found that I could not sensibly distinguish castle from palace, house from hut, roof from ruin. My list embraces any structure in which men and women have laid their heads, provided that they are in some degree accessible to public view. The selection is a personal list and the commentary is a personal vision, warts and all.

Simon Jenkins

Historic houses
of The Midlands

Leicestershire's stock of medieval buildings – Ashby, Kirby Muxloe and Donington – is modest and Leicester's castle hall is inaccessible. Rutland does better with Oakham's Great Hall and its extraordinary horseshoe collection. Leicestershire does have two jewels, both still in their ancestral ownership. One is the immaculate William-and-Mary mansion of Stanford, masterpiece of the Smith family of architects from Warwick. The other is the late Georgian castellated extravaganza of Belvoir, which has been robustly restored and is surrounded by an exotic sculpture garden.

Lincolnshire is one of England's biggest and least-known counties. Medieval wool wealth left it rich in churches but, when that passed, its damp fens and infertile uplands left it poor in houses. From the early Middle Ages is the Jew's House in Lincoln and, from the 15th century, Tattershall, the finest early brick tower in England. Gainsborough's Old Hall is a

little-known but spectacular medieval group. Doddington's prodigy house by Robert Smythson stands guard over Lincoln from the adjacent plain. The Restoration is superbly represented at Lord Brownlow's Belton House. Vanbrugh's Grimsthorpe is one of his most theatrical stage sets, containing a Great Hall to rival Blenheim's. The Georgians are displayed chiefly in the Wyatts' work at Belton. The 19th century left Gregory's astonishing creation by Salvin and Burn at Harlaxton, a revivalist house of a quality unique in England.

Northamptonshire's most distinctive feature is the gloriously rich ironstone of its uplands, yielding houses and villages that look as if made of gingerbread. From the Middle Ages, there is only Rockingham Castle on its bluff and fragments at Nassington and Southwick, but the county is rich in Tudor and Elizabethan houses. Elizabeth's favourite, Christopher Hatton, built two palaces, Kirby and Holdenby, in the hope of receiving her. The former is still an exquisite example of early English Renaissance. Sir Thomas Tresham's pavilions at Rushton and Lyveden are England's most eccentric recusancy designs. More conventional 16th-century mansions are at Fawsley and Deene, still owned by the Brudenells. The 17th century saw one of England's earliest classical mansions at Stoke Park, possibly by Inigo Jones. In the 1630s, the Drydens built their Jacobean range and astonishing ceiling at Canons Ashby. John Webb supplied the Ishams with a classical wing at Lamport and the Spencers inserted the saloon and grand staircase at Althorp. Finally, the 1st Duke of Montagu returned from Paris to replicate a French château at Boughton, laying out miles of formal avenues. James Gibbs built the Great Hall of Kelmarsh, and Smith of Warwick the charming front of Cottesbrooke.

For houses, **Nottinghamshire** is most celebrated for the great ducal estates laid out in the 18th century, mostly by descendants of Bess of Hardwick. Apart from as yet inaccessible Welbeck and Thoresby, these 'Dukeries' have gone. Yet fragments of Nottinghamshire's past survive. Holme Pierrepont remains by the Trent, as does the exterior of Smythson's great showpiece, Wollaton Hall. Handsome gentry houses can be seen at Thrumpton, Papplewick

and Winkburn, the last with unique Georgian relief carvings. Newstead displays the eccentric occupancy of Lord Byron and his respectable Victorian successors. The county is rich in vernacular buildings. The troglodyte caves of Nottingham's sandstone cliffs are rarities. A time warp surrounds the miner's cottage at Eastwood where D.H. Lawrence was born, and Mr Straw's House at Worksop brilliantly evokes early 20th-century life in an English market town.

Warwickshire is blessed with remarkable houses. Two grand castles, Warwick and Kenilworth, lie within its borders. The Elizabethan era is magnificently on show at Aston Hall in Birmingham, at Charlecote and moated Baddesley Clinton. No less impressive are the restored houses linked with Shakespeare in Stratford. In the 18th century Smith of Warwick created Stoneleigh, and Gibbs and James Wyatt the great interiors of Ragley. The Italian plasterers were busy at Ragley and in the remarkable hall and octagon at Honington. The Gothick movement was extrovert in the fan vaults of Arbury. The Victorians were more unobtrusive, with polychrome Ettington the most notable work of Gothic revival. The Elizabethan revival was active at Charlecote and the manorial revival at Packwood. Upton offers an excellent example of modern arts patronage.

✪ STAR RATINGS AND ACCESSIBILITY ✪✪✪✪✪

The 'star' ratings are entirely my personal choice (but see note below). They rate the overall quality of the house as presented to the public, and not gardens or other attractions. On balance I scaled down houses, however famous, for not being easily accessible or for being only partly open.

The top rating, five stars, is given to those houses that qualify as 'international' celebrities. Four stars are awarded to houses of outstanding architectural quality and public display. Three-star houses comprise the run of good historic houses, well displayed and worthy of national promotion. Two and one-star houses are

of more local interest, are hard to visit, or have just one significant feature.

Accessibility varies greatly, from buildings that are open all year to houses that can only be visited 'by appointment' (rarely, I have broken my rule and included a private property that is not open at all, but is viewable from nearby walks or public gardens). Opening hours tend to alter from year to year, but an indication of how accessible a house is to visitors is given at the start of each entry, together with brief information on location and ownership. Many of the houses are National Trust or English Heritage properties, some are now museums or

hotels, others are privately owned by families who open to the public for part of the year (English Heritage grant requirements insist on 28 days minimum). Some owners may, understandably, seek to cluster visitors on particular days. More details for each house are given at the back of this book, and readers are advised to check before visiting.

A final note, houses are, or should be, living things subject to constant change and how we view them is bound to be a subject of debate. I welcome any correction or comment, especially from house owners, sent to me c/o the publisher.

NOTE: On the UK map (pages 6-7) the 4 and 5-star houses in England and Wales were selected by Simon Jenkins. Those in Scotland were selected by Hamish Scott and the editors of Reader's Digest.

Architectural timeline
and Midlands houses in brief

Althorp
First built in the late 16th century, remodelled in the 1660s, with alterations in the 1780s by Henry Holland. Part of the interiors were refashioned in the 19th century.

Arbury Hall
An Elizabethan house transformed in the 18th century with a Gothick-style exterior and interiors decorated with intricate Strawberry-Hill style plasterwork and fan vaulting.

Ashby-de-la-Zouch Castle
Remains of a castle, built in the 15th century more as an ornamental feature than a defensive structure. It includes a substantial fortified tower and medieval kitchen range.

Aubourn Hall
Elizabethan house, three-storeys tall, believed to be influenced by John Smythson, son of Robert. The doorway is a Jacobean addition, as are elements inside.

Baddesley Clinton
A Jacobean manor house built around a courtyard with medieval parts and a moat. It was sympathetically refashioned and restored by its Victorian owners, and the interiors reflect Victorian revival taste.

Belton House
Restoration mansion, once believed to be the work of Christopher Wren but now ascribed to William Winde. The interiors were altered by members of the Wyatt architectural dynasty.

Belvoir Castle
Rebuilt in the early 19th century in a Regency Gothic style, with many towers and turrets. Designed by Matthew Wyatt and other members of that architectural dynasty.

Birmingham: Aston Hall
Mansion built in the early 17th century as a 'prodigy' house to designs by John Thorpe. The southern façade features a loggia, the east front is conventionally Jacobean.

Birmingham: Blakesley Hall
A black-and-white Elizabethan mansion in the city's suburbs. The Great Chamber wing survives, as does Great Hall with gabled rooms over the porch and dias alcove.

Birmingham: Selly Manor
A Tudor manor house rescued and moved to Bournville as a focal point for Cadbury's garden suburb. The solar, in a wing above the parlour, has a rare outside entrance staircase.

Birmingham: Soho House
Georgian house, built in the 1760s by Matthew Boulton, a pioneering industrialist and member of the Lunar Society. The house's innovative features include central heating.

Boughton House
A Tudor manor house built around a courtyard, transformed with a French-style façade in the late 17th century. The palatial interiors include an enfilade of state rooms and superb art.

Canons Ashby
A medieval house extended in the late 15th century around a courtyard. The interiors were remodelled in the 1630s, when the drawing room acquired its domed ceiling, and in the early 18th century.

Charlecote Park
This Elizabethan house, finished in 1558, claims association with Shakespeare; there is a Renaissance-style gatehouse. The house was restored and redecorated in the 19th century.

Coombe Abbey
The remnants of a Cistercian abbey – cloisters windows can still be seen in the court – within a Jacobean mansion with a Restoration wing; later Victorian additions were demolished.

Cottesbrooke Hall
House begun in the 18th century to designs by Francis Smith of Warwick in English Baroque style. The interiors are Georgian, redesigned in an Adam style by Robert Mitchell.

Coughton Court
A Tudor house refashioned in Gothic style in the 1780s by architect John Carter. A fan-vaulted entrance was created in the gatehouse; the interiors reflect a range of eras.

Deene Park
An Elizabethan mansion built around a courtyard on an earlier, 14th-century house. Further rooms were added in the 18th and 19th centuries.

Doddington Hall
A late Elizabethan house attributed to Robert Smythson. Three-storeys tall and topped with three belvederes, it is built in brick. The interiors were modernized in the 1760s.

Donnington-le-Heath Manor House
A medieval hall house dating from around 1290. The hall, open to the roof, stands above an undercroft; wings to the rear form a courtyard. Early windows survive.

Eastwood: D. H. Lawrence House
A two-up, two-down terraced house in a mining village, the birthplace and childhood home of D. H. Lawrence. The house is decorated as it would have been when occupied by Lawrence's parents.

Epworth: The Old Rectory
A red-brick Queen-Anne house with a hipped roof, the childhood home of John Wesley. The rectory was rebuilt after a fire in 1709 from which Wesley was famously saved.

Ettington Park
Victorian mansion built in an early Gothic style and designed by T. F. Pritchard. The exterior is faced with a range of different coloured stone and adorned with sculptures.

Farnborough Hall
A William-and-Mary house altered in the 18th century, probably by William Jones, to reflect Grand Tour influences of its owner. The classical busts are in their original setting.

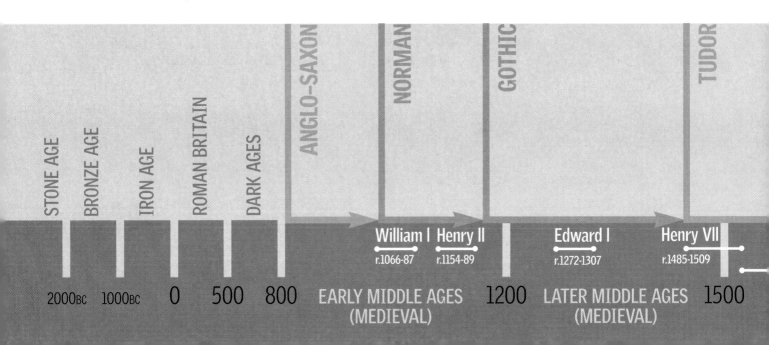

STONE AGE BRONZE AGE IRON AGE ROMAN BRITAIN DARK AGES ANGLO–SAXON NORMAN GOTHIC TUDOR

William I r.1066-87   Henry II r.1154-89   Edward I r.1272-1307   Henry VII r.1485-1509

2000BC 1000BC 0 500 800 EARLY MIDDLE AGES (MEDIEVAL) 1200 LATER MIDDLE AGES (MEDIEVAL) 1500

Fawsley Hall
Elizabethan house with additions made in the 18th century and a wing designed by Anthony Salvin in 1869. The magnificent Great Hall has a restored roof and projecting bay window.

Gainsborough Old Hall
A medieval manor house, reputedly rebuilt in 1484 for a visit by Richard III. The Great Hall, kitchen range and solar chamber survive, along with a suite of royal apartments.

Grimsthorpe Castle
House with 16th-century origins, transformed in 1715 by Sir John Vanbrugh, the architect's last work. The interiors were further altered later in the 18th century and in the 19th.

Gunby Hall
House with William-and-Mary façade, dated to 1700, of red brick with stone. The house was a favourite of James Lees-Milne, the first Historic Buildings Secretary of the National Trust.

Harlaxton Manor
House begun in 1832 in Elizabethan style, with Anthony Salvin as architect. Salvin was replaced by William Burn and the style changed to Jacobean, then Baroque, with a hint of Rococo.

Holdenby House
A Victorian neo-Elizabethan house built on the remains of a once-great, late 16th-century mansion. The original kitchen range survives, as do two gate arches in the grounds.

Holme Pierrepont Hall
A Tudor house with medieval parts, built of red brick. It was once set around several courtyards. Three Tudor ranges survive, with a Victorian wing completing the remaining courtyard.

Honington Hall
A red-brick Restoration mansion, c1682, refashioned in the 1740s and 50s. The interiors were redecorated in Rococo style and include the Octagon, a saloon completed in 1751.

Kelham Hall
Victorian Gothic house by Sir Gilbert Scott with lavish use of Pugin-style details. The exterior features a range of different pointed arches and an Italian Gothic arcade.

Victorian Gothic revival architecture

Victorian architecture drew on many historic styles. Classical architecture from both Rome and Greece influenced taste, but it was medieval style that dominated the design of new buildings. Medieval architecture had been inspiring architects as early as the beginning of the 18th century, but the 'Gothick' style of that era used elements from medieval buildings without attempting to reproduce them faithfully. Motifs were inserted into new buildings for their decorative merits alone. But in the 19th century, architects began to take a more considered archaeological approach and designed whole buildings that were consciously 'medieval'.

Questions of style and taste in art, design and architecture were hotly debated in the 19th century, and the opinions and sensibilities of men such as John Ruskin, A. W. N. Pugin and William Morris were highly influential. For theorists and commentators like these, the Middle Ages was a highpoint in civilization. They rejected classicism as pagan and barbaric, embracing Gothic architecture as the product of a purer, Christian society. Victorian Gothic, therefore, came to have a spiritual dimension and became the style of choice for churches and many significant public buildings, including Pugin and Barry's Houses of Parliament. The style also found favour in domestic architecture and was used for many homes: Gilbert Scott embraced its principles at Kelham Hall (page 108) and T. F. Pritchard adopted Early Gothic for Ettington Park (page 154).

Kelmarsh Hall
Palladian house designed by James Gibbs in the 1730s and built by Smith of Warwick, who employed the Atari brothers as stuccoists. James Wyatt contributed further interiors.

Kenilworth Castle
A Norman castle and medieval palace that was home to Elizabeth I's favourite, the Earl of Leicester. The castle was slighted in the Civil War and its ruins influenced Victorian taste.

Kirby Hall
Ruin of a major Elizabethan mansion, the creation of Sir Christopher Hatton, owner of Holdenby. A frontispiece by Nicholas Stone, pupil of Inigo Jones, was added in the 1630s.

Kirby Muxloe Castle
Begun in the 1470s but left unfinished a few years later, with just a brick gatehouse and a tall corner tower, surrounded by a moat.

Lamport Hall
Built by John Webb in 1654 and extended with flanking wings by Smith of Warwick in the 1730s. Further additions were made later.

Leicester: Belgrave Hall
House built for a Leicester merchant in 1709, now on the outskirts of the city. The simple façade is unadorned brick; the interiors are displayed as 18th-century reconstructions.

Leicester: Newarke Houses
Two Elizabethan or possibly older town houses, close to Leicester Castle. They have been much altered over the centuries, but some fine panelling survives inside.

Lincoln: Jew's House
Stone-built house from around the end of the 12th century in what was the Jewish quarter of medieval Lincoln. Rounded Norman arches can still be seen both outside and in.

Lyddington Bede House
Once a wing of the summer palace of the Bishops of Lincoln, the house was converted into an almshouse in the early 17th century. It features a pentice, or covered walkway.

Lyveden New Bield
The shell of an Elizabethan house, built by Sir Thomas Tresham as a hunting and banqueting lodge, but unfinished at his death in 1605. The exterior is decorated with Catholic symbols.

Marston Hall
Elizabethan house, probably built to an E-plan, with wings and gatehouse later demolished. Greatly modified from the 18th century on.

Middleton Hall
A collection of medieval buildings around a courtyard. The Hall was georgianized in the 18th century. The group is under restoration.

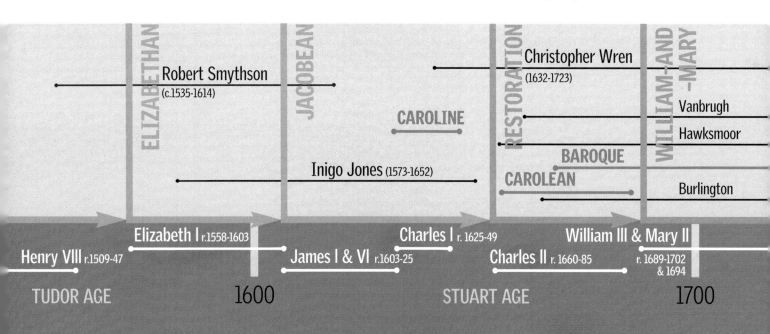

Anthony Salvin (1799-1881)

Born in Co. Durham, Anthony Salvin began his career in 1817, working for architect John Paterson on the restoration of medieval Brancepeth Castle. Salvin moved to London in 1821 where he became the pupil of John Nash before setting up in his own practice. In 1826, he was commissioned to rebuild Mamhead in Devon, where he created a neo-Tudor mansion, with Jacobean and Gothic touches. Throughout his career, Salvin was influenced by Tudor, Elizabethan and Jacobean architecture – Harlaxton Manor (see page 50) and Thoresby Hall (page 121) rate among his finest work – but he also drew on other styles, including Italianate and French.

Some of his most important commissions were to repair and refashion castles – he renovated Norwich, Newark, Rockingham, Alnwick and Warwick, to name but a few. After restoring parts of the Tower of London, he was asked by Prince Albert to undertake work at Windsor Castle. Salvin's success lay in his ability to sympathetically repair the ancient fabric of these buildings, while at the same time creating a comfortable home with modern amenities, such as lighting, heating and plumbing.

Despite suffering a stroke in 1857, while working on Warwick Castle, Salvin did not retire until 1879.

Nassington: Prebendal Manor House
A medieval manor, complete with Great Hall, that claims to date back to the 13th century. It is believed that the house stands on the site of one of King Canute's manors.

Newark Castle
The remains of a Norman castle built on a strategic riverside spot. The gatehouse survives in part, as does the courtyard with curtain wall and outer wall of the Great Hall.

Newstead Abbey
Early 19th-century neo-Gothic mansion created by John Shaw from Byron's family home. The original priory, acquired by the Byrons on the Dissolution, was retained.

Normanby Hall
House built in the 1820s and designed by Robert Smirke in a severe classical style. It was extended over the centuries but by the 1940s was considered too big and was reduced to its current size.

Northampton: Abington Park
A medieval house refashioned in the late 15th century. A new main façade, attributed to Smith of Warwick, was added between 1738 and 1743. The medieval Great Hall remains.

Nottingham: Brewhouse Yard
A row of houses built of red brick beneath the rock of Nottingham Castle and dating from the 1680s. Behind the houses are a set of service quarters cut into the rock.

Nottingham: Wollaton Hall
Elizabethan mansion finished in 1588, designed by Robert Smythson with an astonishing façade and 'prospect room'. The interiors were restored by Wyatville in 1801.

Nottingham: Ye Olde Salutation Inn
An inn first built in the late 12th century. Its current façade dates from the 16th century. Below the pub are a series of caves, once inhabited, that may have prehistoric origins.

Oakham Castle
A Norman Great Hall, the only surviving part of what was once a royal castle The aisled hall features sculpted capitals, rare survivors of Norman art, and its walls are hung with ancient horseshoes.

Packwood House
The home of a Tudor yeoman, restored by a 20th-century industrialist who added new ranges, including a Great Hall. The interiors have features rescued from elsewhere.

Papplewick Hall
Late 18th-century house with a severe Georgian façade. The interiors are decorated in Adam style, with plasterwork that has been attributed to his stuccoist, Joseph Rose.

Ragley Hall
A house begun in 1680 by Robert Hooke, but completed by James Gibbs, and later James Wyatt, in the 18th century. A modern *trompe-l'œil* mural decorates the staircase hall.

Rockingham Castle
A medieval house built within the bailey of a Norman keep, and remodelled and extended in Tudor times. Further sympathetic additions were made by Salvin in the 19th century.

Rushton Triangular Lodge
A most unusual three-sided lodge, built by Sir Thomas Tresham, a Roman Catholic, as a representation of the Holy Trinity. The various architectural components are all based on the number three.

Southwell Workhouse
A workhouse built in 1824 by the Rev John Becher, a social reformer. It was designed with separate accommodation for men, women and children.

Southwick Hall
An Elizabethan hall between two 14th-century towers, survivors of an earlier house. A wing was added in the 18th century. Medieval rooms inside the house remain unaltered.

Spalding: Ayscoughfee Hall
A late medieval house, built for a local wool merchant in the 1450s. It has been added to in almost every era; the exterior was gothicized in the 19th century but retained its medieval structure.

Stanford Hall
House begun by William Smith of Warwick in the 1690s, with further contributions from later Smiths in the next century. The entrance hall was transformed into a ballroom in 1745.

Stapleford Park
A house of many eras; the earliest part, dating from the 1500s, was altered in the 1630s. An Edwardian neo-Elizabethan range was inserted between two 17th-century wings.

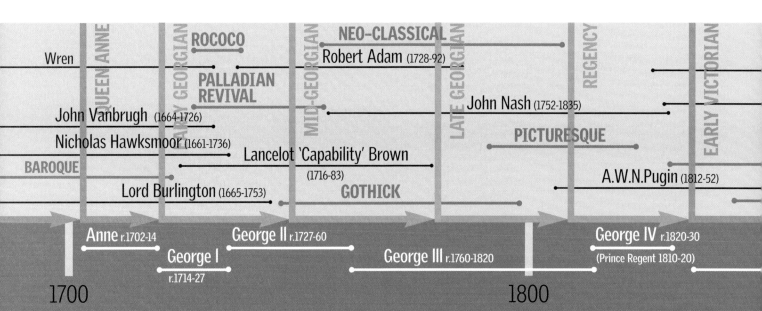

Staunton Harold Hall
A Georgian mansion, part of a complex of house, church and outbuildings, set in wooded parkland. The main façade is of red brick, with a central bay of stone.

Stoke Park
Two pavilions, similar to buildings by Inigo Jones. They were once part of a mansion said to be the first English house in Palladian style.

Stoke Rochford Hall
A Victorian mansion, in Jacobethan-revival style with abundant chimneys and towers. It was built to compete with nearby Harlaxton and designed by that house's second architect, William Burn.

Stoneleigh Abbey
House with main wing by Francis Smith of Warwick, and fragments of the 12th-century monastery. After a fire in 1960, the exterior was repaired by patching with new stone.

Stratford: Anne Hathaway's Cottage
The ultimate chocolate-box English cottage, with half-timbered walls and a deeply thatched roof. Probably dating from the 15th century it was the home of Anne Hathaway before she married Shakespeare.

Stratford: Shakespeare's Birthplace
The house where William Shakespeare was born. Contemporary interiors are re-created within the half-timbered town house, including the workshop of Shakespeare's father.

Stratford: Hall's Croft
Town house built in 1613 by John Hall, a well-to-do physician who was married to Shakespeare's daughter, Susanna. The rooms are furnished with Jacobean pieces and suitably decorated.

Stratford: Mary Arden's House
A farmhouse long supposed to have been the home of Mary Arden, Shakespeare's mother. Recent research suggests another farm nearby was more likely to have been her home.

Stratford: Nash's House
An Elizabethan house, once the home of Thomas Nash, who married Shakespeare's grand-daughter; it once stood next to New Place, the home of Shakespeare's last years.

James Lees-Milne and the National Trust

James Lees-Milne (1908–97) joined the staff of the National Trust in 1936 as secretary to the Country Houses Committee, a newly formed body concerned with the conservation of historic buildings. He was assigned the task of drawing up a list of properties in need of preservation and approaching house owners who might be interested in receiving help from the Trust.

Few houses were acquired before 1939 and in 1940 Lees-Milne joined the army. Invalided out in 1941, he returned to his former job. In the years that followed, as the owners of country houses struggled to maintain their homes, Lees-Milne secured some of the greatest houses in Britain, including Knole, Petworth, Cliveden and Montacute. He tried to make the transfer as easy as possible for both the owners and the Trust – many owners were able to continue living in their homes while upkeep was taken over by the Trust. Lees-Milne also appreciated what he called 'small gems', houses like Gunby Hall (see page 48), which was one of his favourites.

He remained in his post until 1951 but continued working for the Trust in an advisory role. He devoted more time to writing and his diaries provide a remarkable insight into his work in the conservation of some of Britain's finest historic houses.

Sulgrave Manor
A Tudor hall house, rebuilt in both the 18th and 20th centuries. The Great Hall can still be seen. The house was once the home of the Washington family, ancestors of George Washington, first president of the USA.

Tattershall Castle
A brick tower built by Lord Cromwell in the 1430s as part of an already large castle. Though fortified, the tower housed many rooms and was more a residential wing than a defensive structure.

Thoresby Hall
A Jacobethan house, designed by Salvin towards the end of his long career, to replace a mansion by Carr of York. The Great Hall with minstrel's gallery is well preserved.

Thrumpton Hall
A 17th-century mansion, in which the former Great Hall was adapted to be the entrance hall. The gabled façade and magnificent staircase were added in the 1660s. Further alterations were made in the 1800s.

Upton Hall
Regency villa of the 1830s with a simple exterior but finely decorated interiors; the hall rises through the building to a dome. The house is now a museum of clocks.

Upton House
A William-and-Mary hunting lodge extended in the 1920s and transformed by the owners of Shell into a home for their art collection.

Warwick Castle
A magnificent medieval castle, built around a Norman one on a site overlooking the River Avon. The interiors include re-creations from various eras featuring Tussaud's waxworks.

Warwick: Lord Leycester Hospital
Medieval headquarters of the Guilds of Warwick that became an almshouse for the soldiers of the Earl of Leicester. The guild hall and Great Hall can still be seen.

Winkburn Hall
William-and-Mary house built around 1695, reputedly designed by William Smith of Warwick. Inside is fine plasterwork and a set of carved relief panels set above the doors.

Woolsthorpe Manor
The comfortable farmhouse where Isaac Newton was born. The house is simply furnished in 17th-century style.

Worksop: Mr Straw's House
Semi-detached Edwardian suburban villa that was the home of a family of local tradesmen. It remained unchanged from the 1930s and passed intact to the National Trust.

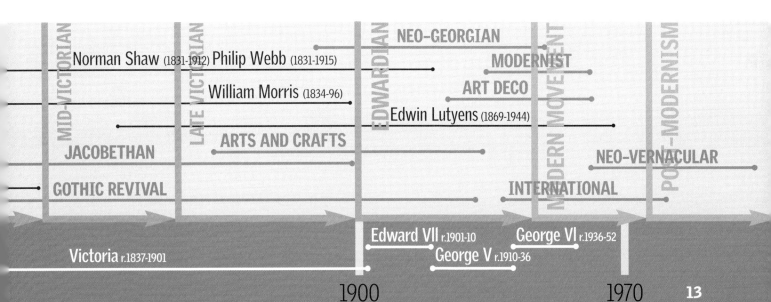

Norman Shaw (1831-1912) Philip Webb (1831-1915)
William Morris (1834-96)
Edwin Lutyens (1869-1944)

MID-VICTORIAN / LATE VICTORIAN / EDWARDIAN / MODERN MOVEMENT / POST-MODERNISM

NEO-GEORGIAN
MODERNIST
ART DECO
ARTS AND CRAFTS
JACOBETHAN
NEO-VERNACULAR
GOTHIC REVIVAL
INTERNATIONAL

Edward VII r.1901-10   George VI r.1936-52
George V r.1910-36

Victoria r.1837-1901

1900   1970   **13**

Belvoir Castle

& Rutland

Leicestershire & Rutland

Ashby-de-la-Zouch castle

⭐ Remains of a 15th-century tower with a medieval kitchen

At Ashby-de-la-Zouch, 12 miles S of Derby; English Heritage, open all year

Powerful men lived dangerously in the 15th century. William Hastings rose to be Lord Chamberlain and close favourite of the Yorkist Edward IV during the Wars of the Roses. He was awarded the Ashby lands of the Lancastrian Earl of Ormonde. In 1474 he applied for permission to fortify the castle there and also his house at Kirby Muxloe (see page 22). Though loyal to the House of York, he was suspected of treachery by Richard III and was beheaded in the Tower in 1483. Muxloe was uncompleted and remained so. Hastings' descendants were no more fortunate during the next Civil War. They held Ashby for the King and saw it slighted in 1649. The slighting can still be seen, the keep and kitchen being sapped with explosives.

Ashby Castle is impressive, as if wrecked only yesterday. The most dramatic ruin is of Hastings' ornamental 'pretend-keep', a huge structure for its day. It stands apart from the earlier medieval castle ruins. Such towers were for show, like Ralph Cromwell's Tattershall (see page 59). It stands proud, four storeys high, shorn only of its top battlements. Beneath are the remains of four floors of grand rooms with spacious windows, chopped clean in half by the slighting. One window has a charming ogee canopy. There are polygonal corner turrets with pilasters. This must have been a medieval fantasy tower of the sort the Victorians spent fortunes re-creating. Why cannot we restore this original one? It is purely a matter of courage.

The spiral staircase survives and leads to the roof, unless the health-and-safety gnomes have closed it. Of the remainder of the castle, the footings of the chapel and priest's house can be seen. The best survival is, oddly, the kitchen range which predates Hastings's work. It is one of the biggest medieval kitchens extant, comparable with Glastonbury, in Somerset. Inside can be seen the fireplaces with flues, spaces for cauldrons, ovens and serving hatches. Spiral staircases lead to blocked doors and upper chambers. All trace of life has gone but mystery remains.

Belvoir castle

 A Regency Gothic castle of many towers

At Belvoir, 7 miles W of Grantham; private house, open part year

If the monarch visits Belvoir, the key is handed over not by its owner, the Duke of Rutland, but by the local Staunton family, its ancestral keepers. As manorial rent to the Rutlands, the Stauntons are charged with defending the tower with their lives. Such are the privileges of dukedom.

Tradition hangs about Belvoir like the cedars and creepers that guard its scenic approach. Leather water buckets protect the inhabitants against fire, and muskets stand ready against rebellion. Yet Belvoir is not a real castle but a 19th-century fantasy. The place is faintly institutional, stacked with military regalia, ancient custodians and, on my visit, an unappetizing smell of school food. It is not so much ducal as regimental.

Belvoir (pronounced beever) has been the home of the Manners family since Tudor times. It was an ancient stronghold on a bluff, rebuilt by the Earls of Rutland in the 16th century. The castle was demolished after the Civil War and rebuilt in 1668 by John Webb. This house was in the process of being altered by Matthew Wyatt when, in 1816, a fire destroyed almost all of what remained of the 17th-century building, also consuming works by Titian, van Dyck and Reynolds. What is seen today is a monument to the architectural Wyatts.

Four of the family served Belvoir, aided by two amateurs, Elizabeth, Duchess of Rutland at the time of the Regency rebuilding, and her chaplain, Sir John Thoroton. Elizabeth was an enthusiastic amateur architect. The result is a Regency Gothic castle in the manner of Windsor or Arundel.

'From **every battlement** we expect **a knight** to wave a banner or **a lady to sob for love.**'

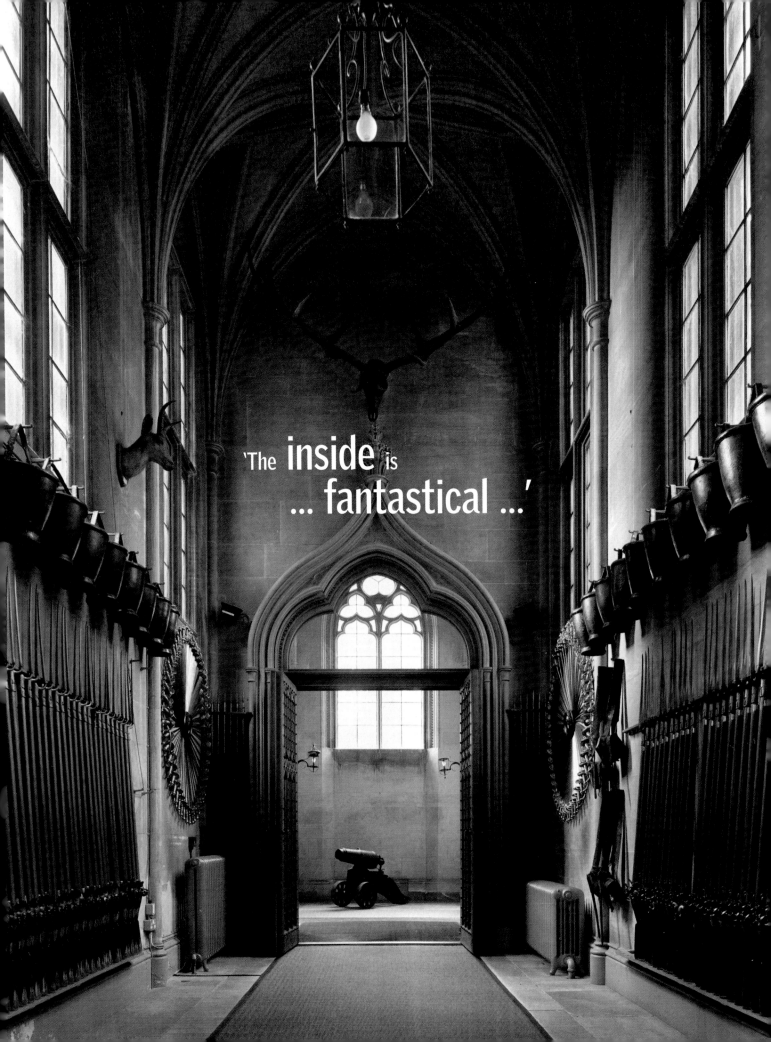

'The **inside** is
... fantastical ...'

Left An enormous elk's head, found in an Irish bog, hangs above the entrance to the long passage known as the pre-guardroom. Leather fire buckets and muskets line the walls; each bucket is decorated with the coronet and cipher of the Dukes of Rutland.
Right Belvoir boasts two Regency Gothic libraries, both designed by Sir John Thoroton. The larger of the two features a ceiling decorated with the arms of the Manners family. A portrait of the 5th Duke, presented to him by estate tenants in 1856, hangs over the fireplace.
Below The Elizabeth Saloon was created for Elizabeth, the 5th Duchess. Her likeness can be seen in portraits on the ceiling and in a marble statue.

The entry is up a long avenue which passes sweeping lawns and long views over the Vale of Belvoir below. The castle itself is massive, built in soft ochre ironstone. The exterior is composed of variations on a tower theme. One tower is square, another round, another apparently lozenge-shaped. Others are octagonal with Gothic pinnacles. Some windows are Gothic, some 17th century. Chimneys look like towerlets and vice versa. From every battlement we expect a knight to wave a banner or a lady to sob for love.

The inside is no less fantastical, a variety of Gothic, French, Italian and even Chinese. Thoroton, working possibly to Matthew Wyatt's design, produced an impressive entrance sequence of Gothic chambers with rib-vaults, stone floors, muskets, banners and fire buckets. The guardroom looks ready to explode. A troop of horse could ride upstairs, where they would be greeted with a cavalry museum and a ballroom on the landing. An eternity of Manners' faces look down from the walls.

The style now changes abruptly. The formal tour goes not into the reception rooms but into the Chinese Rooms. These are decorated with 18th-century hand-woven silk. A domed bed, drooping with fabric, might be from a Gothic romance. The chinoiserie is exquisite, the more enjoyable for being old and apparently much in need of restoration. Opposite is another contrast, the Elizabeth

Above The Gothic-style guardroom, designed by Matthew Wyatt, forms the entrance hall of Belvoir. Its walls bristle with arms and armour, including Brown Bess muskets and circles of short swords, known as 'hangers'. These were once wielded by the Leicestershire Militia, of which the 4th Duke became colonel during the American War of Independence.

Saloon by Matthew Wyatt. This is the ladies' withdrawing room, French and shimmering in reds and golds. The 5th Duchess is sculpted in marble. On the ceiling ladies play with peacocks and putti. Ebony cabinets line the walls. The panelling is from a French chateau. Everywhere is gilded plasterwork with crimson hangings. This is the room that the envious Gregory sought to reproduce in neighbouring Harlaxton (see page 50).

The adjacent dining room is no less grand, with a deep coffered ceiling of gilded flower patterns, each one different. Over the mantelpieces are two Manners portraits by Reynolds. The picture gallery contains the finest paintings to survive the fire, including works by Poussin, Teniers, Steen, Gainsborough and a splendid Holbein of Henry VIII. They are relics of one of England's greatest private collections. In the middle of the room, incongruously encased in glass, is the Queen Anne Bed, brought from the Rutlands' other seat, Haddon Hall, in Derbyshire. It is of sumptuous craftsmanship, but there is something sad in an unused bed, a true sleeping beauty.

The King's Rooms, decorated for George IV, resume the chinoiserie, with yellow drapery and pretty hand-painted wallpaper. An entire wing of the castle is occupied by the Regent's Gallery, filled with pictures and furniture and with spectacular views over the Vale. Here are more Rutland treasures, the Gobelins tapestries of Don Quixote acquired by the 5th Duke in Paris in 1814. To one side is a table designed for a version of cat's cradle.

The large and small libraries were by Thoroton in Regency Gothic style. They have ecclesiastical window frames and the customary busts of emperors and philosophers. The family chapel contains paintings by Murillo and Bassano and effigies of monks. The castle grounds are occupied by often startling examples of modern sculpture, an admirable innovation.

Donington-le-Heath
manor house

⭐ Medieval hall house dating from the late 13th century

At Donington-le-Heath, 12 miles NW of Leicester; museum, open all year

The area between Leicester and Derby is as grim as any in England, a wilderness of giant sheds and dreary estates with a feel neither for history nor contour. Yet it has surprises. One is this medieval hall house, besieged with gravel and municipal lawn. It claims to be the oldest house in Leicestershire.

The building dates from *c*1290, when it consisted of a hall above an undercroft, with wings to the rear. These now compose a courtyard which, apart from the glazed windows, appears authentically medieval. Numerous original lancet windows have survived, along with early 17th-century casements. If the exterior had not been scrubbed ferociously after being used as a pigsty in the 1950s, it would even be atmospheric.

Ryedale Folk Museum, in Yorkshire, has shown how medieval rooms can be re-created with some truth-to-life. The sparkling white walls, polished floors and modern display cases at Donington-le-Heath are a parody of antiquity. There is some good Jacobean furniture in the hall which is open to the roof. Part of the garden has been laid out as an ancient parterre. There are strange statues in the garden and some welcome bee-hives.

Kirby Muxloe castle

⭐ The gatehouse and corner tower of an unfinished 15th-century castle

At Kirby Muxloe, 4 miles W of Leicester; English Heritage, open part year

For a minute, the Leicestershire sprawl draws back and the eye blots out the estates. By blessed chance – and for how long? – a meadow supplies the backdrop to the old Hastings castle. Set on a grassy rectangle inside a restored moat, this might be the crumbled relic of an Indian Mughal fort.

Kirby Muxloe was begun in 1474 under licence by Lord Hastings, as was the fortification of his other castle at Ashby-de-la-Zouch (see page 16). That was a fantasy castle, this was a fortified house. Work did not start until 1480 but, since Hastings fell from grace three years later, was never completed. Unlike Ashby, Kirby Muxloe is of brick, beautifully laid with diaper patterning and a pleasure to the eye. This was intended to be as fine as any house of its day in England.

What stands is a symmetrical gatehouse, one of the first to have gunports for firing small cannon at attackers, and a high corner tower. The gatehouse is most impressive when approached over its bridge across the moat. It has projecting bays, the gunports in them looking like drains. Since the upper floors were not completed we must assume that the upper walls would have enclosed a large chamber over the entrance. The Great Hall would have been on the far side of the courtyard. The panel over the entrance still awaits the Hastings arms, not being incised before his execution.

The corner tower has three storeys and was finished. It is battlemented and has an exciting spiral staircase of brick leading to the roof. The rooms are what would now be called en suite, with their own garderobes dropping into the basement, where the nightsoil would have been collected. Here, too, are small gunports, surely as dangerous for their users as for their victims.

LEICESTER
Belgrave hall

★ Early Georgian home of a prosperous city merchant

Church Road, Belgrave, Leicester; museum, open part year

The enclave of Belgrave Hall on the outskirts of Leicester is precious. The old house is early Georgian begun in 1709, its façade eerily puritanical. A narrow entrance of three bays is recessed behind two wings, each with five identical windows on three floors. There are no quoins, no parapet, no adornment. The back (shown above), apart from the three gables to the third floor, is as simple. All this was built by a rich merchant in the age of John Vanbrugh.

The house was the home and headquarters of the Vann family, Leicestershire hosiers. Their descendants sold it to Leicester City Council in 1936, from whom it passed to the county. The interior has been refurnished and is refreshingly free of museumitis. The waxworks are decorous and the rooms, if rather bare, reflect the undemonstrative comfort of a prosperous family of the period. Nothing is spectacular.

The ground floor plan is strange. The kitchen is where we might expect a drawing room, close to the dining room across the hall. Was this meanness or did the Vanns like their food hot? The dining room has columns to the bay window, with crude Corinthian capitals. The staircase has fine twisted balusters. On the first floor are the drawing room, a bedroom, bathroom and parlour. In the last a stuffed cat plays with a ball of wool. The top floor is for the nursery and housekeeper's room. Walled gardens survive at the back.

Newarke houses

✦ Two Elizabethan town houses, much altered over the years

The Newarke, Leicester; museum, open all year

Crouching in the backwash of a domineering Leicester gyratory traffic scheme is a fragment of the old city next to the castle and river. The castle includes reputedly the longest Great Hall in England, that of the Earl of Leicester's 1351 hospital. It is not regularly open to the public, unimaginable in any other city in Europe. Instead, we are allowed to see two town houses in The Newarke outside. A fragment of medieval wall survives in their garden.

The two houses were once Skeffington House and Wyggeston's Chantry. They are Elizabethan or older in origin and traces of this can be seen on the exterior, in gables with ball finials and a few old windows. The insides have been so altered over the years and recently knocked about by the museum as to be barely 'old'. Yet there are three fine panelled rooms, one of them spectacularly rich, with lozenge panels and pilasters and appropriate furniture. The staircase is 18th century and has portraits of the period on the walls. In the upstairs Long Room is a charming overmantel of 1631. This was rescued from Ragdale Old Hall, a Leicestershire Tudor mansion scandalously demolished in 1958 at the time when English houses suffered the equivalent of the Black Death.

As a museum, the Newarke Houses are full of oddities. There are dozens of clocks, including a display of how they were made. There is also an excellent fake street to the rear and a museum of one of Leicester's favourite sons, Daniel Lambert. At 53 stone, he is still unbeaten as 'the fattest man in England'. He was keeper of the local jail in the 18th century.

Lyddington Bede house

★★ Fragment of a bishop's palace that became an almshouse

At Lyddington, 6 miles N of Corby; English Heritage, open part year

The house was once part of a summer palace of the Bishops of Lincoln. The range was built in the mid-15th century and passed at the Dissolution to Lord Burghley, who converted it to almshouses in *c*1600. That use survived until the 1930s. It seems a pity that it cannot still serve that purpose, at least in part.

The Bede House sits next to the church, built of the same astonishingly rich, honey-coloured ironstone in which this part of England abounds. The grey ashlar dressings and buttresses seem an impertinence to this superb material. At the time of conversion in the 16th century, Tudor windows were inserted into the main walls upstairs while smaller windows light the bedesmen's cells downstairs. Tall chimneys indicate creature comforts. Along the north side is a wooden pentice, a walkway for sheltered promenading which was much favoured by Tudor almshouses, such as those at Abingdon, in Oxfordshire.

The bedesmen's cells are in what would have been an open undercroft beneath the Great Chamber. They offer a fascinating relic of an ancient old people's home, tiny but neat, warm and secure. They must have seemed luxurious to those whose lives had been spent in the fields and hovels of the village. Above is the Bishop's Presence Chamber, survivor of the old palace, and a smaller private room. This is where the bishop would have received petitioners and conducted local business on his visits. It is ceiled with wood and has unusual coving carved in imitation of fan vaulting. There is painted glass in the windows.

Oakham castle

★ A Norman Great Hall, once part of a significant castle

At Oakham, 9 miles SE of Melton Mowbray; museum, open all year

All that survives of the royal castle of Oakham is its Great Hall. The rest is a series of lumps, dips and mounds in the park, precious to archaeologists and children but no one else. The hall is reached down a charming alleyway from the market square and is one of the most spectacular domestic interiors to survive anywhere from the Norman era.

From the outside, one might be looking at a conventional church hall, with aisles and dormer windows. Inside, an aisled hall rises to a kingpost roof. The arches on each side are divided by piers, with superb Norman sculptures for capitals. These would be remarkable in a church and are exceptionally rare in a secular building. We see the heads of kings and queens, animals and musicians, some with their instruments still discernible. The carving has been related to 12th-century work at Canterbury Cathedral and indicates the early prominence of Oakham on the route north.

A quite different matter is the astonishing decoration of horseshoes covering every inch of the walls. They look at first like the collection of some obsessive schoolboy. The horseshoes are of differing size and materials. All are hung upside down, despite the tradition that horseshoes should be kept upright to prevent the luck falling out. Some are gigantic, a yard across.

The horseshoes carry the names and arms of visiting peers and royalty who were required to donate a horseshoe or its monetary equivalent to the lord of the Manor of Oakham. The custom is first mentioned in the 16th century, although the oldest is claimed to date from 1470. There are some 200 in all, many more having been thrown out by the Victorians, and lost.

Stanford hall

★ ★ ★   A late 17th-century house by Smith of Warwick, with fine interiors

At Stanford on Avon, 7 miles NW of Rugby; private house, open part year

Stanford is the perfect William-and-Mary house. When seen from the road, the south front floats like a palace of romance across a distant meadow. Two tiers of windows are set in pale stone walls beneath a protective hipped roof.

The property has belonged since 1430 to the Cave family, now represented by Lady Braye, a lineage celebrated in the superb memorial in the local church. The architect of the present house was William Smith, the older Smith of Warwick, in that most exquisite of decades, the 1690s. Younger members of his family georgianized the east front, making it the entrance, and built the stables.

Inside, each room is a gem, enhanced by evidence of continuous family occupation. Everything seems in regular use and not merely 'on display'. The front entrance leads not into a hall but unusually into one end of a long passage. This is the result of the original entrance hall having been made into the ballroom in 1745.

Immediately to the left is the panelled library, displaying historical documents and accounts for the original building. A family Bible was embroidered in silk in 1629 by a Cave daughter in thanks

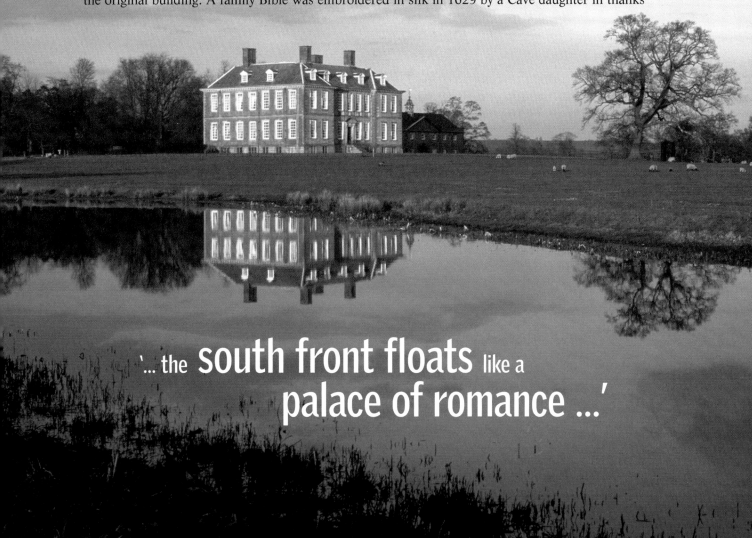

'... the **south front floats** like a **palace of romance** ...'

Above In the Green Drawing Room a portrait of Henrietta Maria hangs over the fireplace. It was painted at the time of her engagement to Charles I. **Above right** The library holds a collection of around 5,000 books, dating back to the 17th century. **Right** A 17th-century tapestry depicting a Roman battle hangs on the west wall of the South East Bedroom. The four-poster bed is Victorian.

for having survived the lustful advances of the Pasha on a visit to Turkey. A Georgian silhouette, *The Quintet* by F. Torond, depicts the 5th Baronet, his wife and three friends playing musical instruments.

The ballroom was created by the younger Smith with a flamboyance worthy of a Viennese palace. The deeply coved ceiling has giant *trompe-l'œil* scallops in each corner while the central roundel depicts Apollo in a sunburst. It is a sensational composition. Doorway and overmantel are sumptuous, bold pink with heavy gilding. Most of the paintings are of the Stuarts, their Pretenders and courtiers, acquired as a lot by Lady Braye in Rome in 1842 during a burst of Stuart revivalist fervour. They include a rare portrait of Bonnie Prince Charlie in exile at the age of fifty.

The Green and Grey Drawing Rooms have more paintings of Stuarts. In the former is a magnificent black cat of Staffordshire pottery and an unusual German cabinet inlaid with Persian hunting scenes. Over the Grey Drawing Room mantelpiece is a masterful flower painting by Bosschaert. It outshines a copy of van Dyck's royal children on the adjacent wall. The Old Dining Room is hung with Tudor and other portraits set amid the most brilliant crimson damask wall-hangings.

A spacious Georgian staircase hall fills the core of the house. It has triple balusters and is hung with Cave portraits of all periods. The upstairs bedrooms are admirably cluttered. In the Bachelor's Room – so called for being 'too dark for a lady' – is a pleasing contrast of fabrics. A Flemish tapestry covers a wall, the four-poster has a 19th-century pelmet and the bed an American quilt. Stanford is in good hands.

Stapleford park

 A much-altered mansion with additions from many different dates

At Stapleford, 4 miles E of Melton Mowbray; now a hotel

The first owners of Stapleford were old money, the Earls of Harborough. They held it for four centuries. The next owners were new money, the brewing Grettons, who held it for one century. Since 1982 it has changed hands repeatedly and is now a luxury hotel. Novelty is regularly proclaimed, the latest being 'an executive chef who is spiking his cuisine with light fresh flavours'.

Stapleford was acquired by the Sherard family, Earls of Harborough, in 1402 and a new house built by 1500. One wing of this survives and holds the chief architectural interest of the building. It was embellished by Lady Abigail Sherard in 1633 with extravagant Dutch gables and Gothic niches, considered early examples of Gothic revivalism. In its appearance it is 'reminiscent of Flemish town halls', said Pevsner. Six of the twelve niches purport to show Sherard ancestors, making it more likely that this was calculated antiquarianism, like Lady Anne Clifford's work in the Borders at the same time.

The rest of the present house was built in a U-shape onto the back of the old house, facing the park. It is of the late 17th century, of two storeys with a boldly hipped roof. The present hotel entrance front is of this date, but on the far side we can see that the house was drastically altered by the Grettons at the end of the 19th century. A modern, neo-Elizabethan block was crudely inserted between the two arms of the U. The result looks like an Edwardian swell with a lady on each arm.

As a result it is near impossible to date the interior. The entrance leads to a Victorian hall with a bold stone balcony, heavily decorated with trophies and paintings of stags. Many of the reception rooms retain 17th-century ceilings and fittings, notably the 'Grinling Gibbons' overmantel and doorcases in the dining room, moved from the original saloon upstairs. Lord Gretton allegedly rebuilt the house to advance his social position in the county. He should have let the 17th century do it unaided.

Staunton Harold hall

⭐ A Georgian mansion set in sylvan parkland

At Staunton Harold, 7 miles S of Derby; private house, open by arrangement

Glimpsed amid thick woods from the Ashby to Melbourne road is the epitome of old England. Lying in the valley below is a curving lake with, amid cedars, an old mansion, church, stables and outbuildings, arrayed as if for a chocolate box. This was the seat of the Shirleys, later Earls Ferrers. The church, now owned by the National Trust, was built during the Commonwealth and its defiant Shirley builder eventually died in the Tower of London.

By the 1950s the Ferrers could not manage the building and it fell into disrepair. It became first a Cheshire Home, then a Sue Ryder hospice, and sadly institutionalized. In 2003 the house was sold to the Blunt family, of Clifton Hall in Staffordshire, to become once again a private residence. The grounds, church, walled gardens and former stables are open to the public and the Blunts offer guided tours of the house to groups. In 1974 the stableblock was converted into workshops for artists and craftsmen, whose skills have been harnessed in the restoration of the house and parkland.

The exterior of the hall is serenely Palladian, built piecemeal over the 18th century, with a north front of *c*1700 and a formal east front looking out over the park. Its façade was designed by the 5th Earl in 1763. There are just two storeys. The three central bays are of stone, the rest of beautifully laid red brick. The nether regions of the house are a warren of rooms, passages and courtyards.

'... the epitome of old England.'

Lincoln

Belton House

shire

Lincolnshire

Aubourn hall

☆ An unusual Elizabethan house, possibly influenced by the younger Smythson

At Aubourn, 7 miles SW of Lincoln; private house, gardens open by arrangement

Aubourn is an odd Elizabethan house of brick, very tall and said to be influenced by John Smythson, son of Robert. The Neviles, who still live here, employed Smythson junior in Nottinghamshire and Robert's biographer, Mark Girouard, remarks that 'this attractive but puzzling house or fragment of a house' seems to show Smythson influence. It sits quietly in a pleasant garden outside Lincoln, with the River Witham for company.

The front is high and asymmetrical with almost square windows, distinctly Elizabethan. The doorway is Jacobean and the inside offers Elizabethan and Jacobean in confusing profusion. The study chimneypiece, of tiered pilasters, is Elizabethan Renaissance. The staircase, pride of the house, is clearly later. It has elongated newel posts and pendants, each fashioned from a single piece of wood. The serpents and foliage are what Pevsner calls 'Gothic-Viking' in style.

The baluster panels are of flat geometrical strapwork, plain yet handsome. The stairs rise two storeys to the top of the house, indicating the increased importance of upper chambers, whether for guests or servants, in the 17th century. At the foot is a superb carved wooden gate to keep dogs, or possibly children, from going upstairs.

34

Belton

★ ★ ★ ☆ Carolean mansion altered by the Wyatt dynasty in the 18th century

3 miles NE of Grantham; National Trust, open part year

Belton is the perfect Restoration house, well mannered yet a little frigid. The ancestral owners, the Brownlows, were Elizabethan lawyers who always did the right thing but never set the Thames on fire. I cannot imagine a Brownlow galloping into the Saloon at Belton and decapitating the porcelain. Inter-war Brownlows were friends of Edward VIII during the Abdication crisis. The King had stayed at Belton with Mrs Simpson and it was a Lord Brownlow who persuaded her, in a letter from France, to renounce him and let him remain king. The letter arrived too late.

The exterior of 1684 was once believed to be by Christopher Wren. It has a deep-pitched roof, dormer windows and white-painted balustrade with cupola, typical of Wren's work. The building material is a rich, honeyed limestone. Belton is now attributed to William Winde, architect of Ashdown, in Oxfordshire, but most of the interiors were altered in the late-Georgian era by various Wyatts. The pleasure of the house thus lies in distinguishing the robust 17th century from the more effete 18th.

'... the **perfect Restoration house,**
well mannered yet a little **frigid.'**

Above The original ceiling in the saloon was replaced in 1811 by Francis Bernasconi. This ceiling fell down in 1877 and was replaced in the 1890s with plasterwork by George Jackson & Sons. Right The early 18th-century bed in the Blue Bedroom was recovered in 1813 with blue silk damask. It was probably converted from a four-poster to an 'angel tester' at around the same time. Far right Once a dressing room, the ante-library was created in 1876, at the same time as the library. Its shelves now hold some of Belton's finest porcelain, including 18th-century Chinese, Japanese and English ware.

The Marble Hall is early, balancing the saloon behind. The two rooms almost cheat the eye, offering vistas through from the formal garden on one side to the landscaped park on the other. The hall has stone floors and limewood carving, some of it attributed to Grinling Gibbons. Paintings and porcelain here, as throughout the house, are superlative. The former include Lelys, Reynolds and Romneys of the Brownlow and related Cust families.

The saloon is more ornamental. Here boots are metaphorically removed and Aubusson covers the floor. The style is still 17th century, with heavy doorcases and ornate plaster ceiling. Again some carvings are probably by Gibbons. The overmantel surround has so many birds it looks as if it might take flight. Next door is the Tyrconnel Room, with a painted floor and carved frieze panel not by Gibbons but by his contemporary, Edmund Carpenter.

The east wing of the house comprises a chapel, complete with family gallery and withdrawing room, surviving from the original house. The guide says the chapel is here 'a quasi-public room of state', its opulence 'arising much from the desire to express status as from more spiritual motives'. Its Baroque reredos is worthy of a City of London church. Exquisite limewood carving surrounds a Flemish Madonna in the chapel gallery.

The remainder of Belton is immaculately displayed. The bed in the Blue Bedroom downstairs has a backing like a majestic organ case. The staircase has wall panels by Jeffry Wyatville and ceilings by Edward Goudge. Lord Leighton's sublime portrait of Lady Brownlow gazes down from on high. The upstairs bedrooms have canopied beds, with hand-painted wallpaper in the Chinese Room. The birds and butterflies are cut-outs added by hand. Pride of place on the first floor goes to the library

Above The Hondecoeter Room has three large canvases by Melchior Hondecoeter (1636–95); the painting over the fireplace is by his cousin, Jan Weenix the Younger. Left The Old Kitchen was abandoned in the 20th century. The Trust has preserved its original 19th-century features and re-created others.

and ante-library. The latter contains a collection of mostly Japanese and Chinese porcelain. In the library is a quaint exercise chair on which the user was expected to bounce. The adjacent boudoir has the finest of the James Wyatt ceilings, every bit the measure of his rival, Robert Adam. Next door is the Windsor Bedroom, in which 'they' presumably stayed. It displays photographs of the couple and a flurry of Cust portraits.

Belton is left through the Tapestry Room, designed to display four Mortlake tapestries depicting the story of Diogenes. The room appears 17th century but is a Victorian re-creation. In a corner of the ground floor is the Hondecoeter Room, designed by Wyatville to take three large paintings by the Dutch artist. They bring indoors the rural scenery which 17th-century landowners across Northern Europe were seeking to create outside, packed with flora and exotic fauna drawn from the new continents of Dutch colonization.

Doddington hall

★ ★ ★ Elizabethan mansion, with interiors converted in the 18th century

At Doddington, 5 miles W of Lincoln; private house, open part year

There are really two Doddingtons. The house appears from the road as an Elizabethan prodigy mansion. Its romantic exterior has three belvedere cupolas, large and serene when seen across a lawn beyond a gatehouse. The tableau is immaculate. The inside is quite different, a Georgian house conversion of 1760.

The Hall was built *c*1600 by Thomas Tailor, Registrar to the Diocese of Lincoln, which then stretched from here to the Thames. Tailor was a lawyer and therefore rich. From the roof of the house, the towers of Lincoln Cathedral are proprietorially visible. Despite a lack of documentary evidence, the house is attributed to Robert Smythson.

It passed down the generations to the Hussey and Delaval families: the latter, of Seaton Delaval Hall in Northumberland, were reputed to have been cursed that they would have no male heirs. Such curses tend to be remembered only when they turn out to be true. When Sarah Hussey's daughter and heir married a Delaval in 1724, she entailed the estate never to be joined to Seaton Delaval. Her Delaval grandson, Sir John, added Hussey to his name. The house passed to George Jarvis, whose descendants live there to this day.

Above At one end of the Long Gallery hangs a portrait by Sir Joshua Reynolds, *The Earl and Countess of Mexborough attending the Coronation of George III*; the Countess was the favourite sister of Sir John Hussey. **Right** The decoration of the drawing room is still much as it would have been after Sir John's modernization, although the flock wallpaper is a copy of the original. Sir John was one of 12 children and portraits of the large family are displayed on the walls.

The exterior is symmetrical and finely proportioned, three storeys of brick with stone quoins. Two wings embrace a façade punctuated by three projecting towers, one for the porch, the others occupying the angles of the wings. Above are hexagonal belvederes with cupolas. The only classical detail is the doorway, topped by Jacobean scrollwork. Despite its impressive façade, Doddington is only one room deep.

The interior can seem a disappointment. Smythson's large rooms – the house had only nine bedrooms – invited modernization rather than demolition when Sir John Hussey Delaval restored the interiors in the 1760s. The Great Hall has lost its screens passage but still extends, medieval fashion, to one side of the porch. The broken pediments of its panelling are adorned with blue-and-white china. Portraits chart the story of the Hussey, Delaval and Jarvis families.

The house's plan has the kitchens and offices to one side of the entrance and the family wing to the other. The latter contains just two rooms on each floor. The library and parlour downstairs are crowded with portraits and china and are in regular family use. They are divided by a grand staircase, beautifully carpentered but rather dull. At its foot is a Reynolds of a glamorous Delaval who raided St Malo in 1758. He swam ashore ahead of his ship and completed the 'conquest' of the undefended port by getting drunk in a bar.

One of the first floor bedrooms, the Tiger Room, has a bed from Seaton Delaval in which the 'Butcher' Duke of Cumberland slept on his way to the Battle of Culloden. He was apparently 5 feet tall but 23 stone in weight, near incredible proportions. Hence the bed steps. The drawing room, formerly the Great Chamber over the Great Hall, has more Delavals and more china, a speciality of Doddington. The chess set was carved from mutton bones by Napoleonic prisoners in the care of a Jarvis ancestor commanding Dover Castle.

The upper floor comprises a Long Gallery running the length of the house. It once had windows on both sides, now bricked up to give more space for hanging pictures. Although the paintings generally are of no great quality, a superb Reynolds fills an end wall. It was sold to the nation in lieu of tax and allowed to remain here 'on loan' provided there is public access, an admirable system.

Epworth: The Old Rectory

⯨ ⯨ The childhood home of John Wesley, rebuilt after a famous fire

Rectory Street, Epworth; museum, open part year

The Reverend Samuel Wesley arrived as Rector of Epworth in 1697. It was a time when Baptists were rioting and threatening all manifestations of the Established church. Wesley was a High Churchman and Royalist, immediately in conflict with the Nonconformist temper of his parish. In 1702 the Rectory was damaged by fire and in 1709 was burnt to the ground. The family of eight children were in bed, but escaped before the roof collapsed.

The last to be rescued from an upstairs window was the six-year-old John, his mother regarding his salvation as being by the hand of God. He was 'a brand plucked from the burning'. That brand, John Wesley, came near to destroying the same Church of England that his father had so bravely upheld. When old Wesley died, his epitaph stated that 'as he lived, so he died in the true Catholic faith'. The young Wesley never rejected that faith and always maintained that his was the true Reformation Anglicanism. This was not how his followers saw it.

Epworth Rectory was rebuilt and often visited by John Wesley during his travels. By the 1950s it was decrepit, and was offered by the diocese to the World Methodist Council. It was opened as a museum in 1957 and is now a Wesleyan shrine. The depiction of young John Wesley's rescue from the fire became one of the most popular of all Victorian engravings.

The rectory is still recognizably the Queen Anne house in which the Wesleys lived. It is a genial box of seven bays by four, the roof gabled at one end and hipped at the other. The interior is simple but not poor. In the entrance stands a Jacobean sideboard and furniture more Methodist than 'High Church' in taste. There is a schoolroom in which 'the incomparable Susanna' Wesley taught her ten surviving children, including John and his young follower, Charles. She determined to 'take such a proportion of time as I can spare every night, to discourse with each child apart'. John had Thursday, Charles Saturday. The girls had to share. On the Queen Anne staircase is the picture of the fire. The attic contains an exhibition of Wesleyana, with much commemorative Staffordshire pottery.

Gainsborough Old hall

★★ A medieval and Tudor hall house, surviving remarkably intact

At Gainsborough, 12 miles S of Scunthorpe; English Heritage, open all year

For once the hyperbole is justified. 'One of the country's best preserved medieval manors', says the guidebook. Gainsborough Old Hall is set on a lawn in a back street behind a dull town centre. It comprises a 15th-century manor with tower, Great Hall, kitchen range, solar and extensive suite of state rooms. Anywhere but in Lincolnshire, the place would be famous.

The house was reputedly rebuilt by Sir Thomas Burgh after a fire, to entertain Richard III in 1484. The property passed to the Hickman family, under whom it became a factory, Congregational chapel, ballroom and auction house, each use saving it from destruction. The Old Hall was given to the nation in 1970.

The building is a textbook of medieval architecture. The Great Hall fills the centre of an H-plan. The hall range is timbered, with lath and plaster, except for a church-like stone projection for the bay window, with traceried openings. The wings are of brick, enclosing a three-sided courtyard to the south.

The interior is remarkably intact, its sensational Great Hall open to a roof of sweeping trusses. There is no chimney and the lantern remains above what would have been a smoke louvre. At one end are the kitchens which have huge fireplaces, and a complete suite of pantry, buttery, bakery and, up ladders, the servants' quarters.

The other end of the Great Hall leads to a Tudor staircase built round a massive newel post. This rises to a gallery and the surviving solar chamber. Beyond in the east wing are the state rooms prepared to welcome the monarch. These include an Upper Great Chamber, with bedrooms on either side. They contain original fireplaces and furniture gathered from the Tudor period, although the ceiling was raised to form a Victorian ballroom. A bedroom in the tower has been restored with wall-hangings. What a survival!

Grimsthorpe castle

✦✦✦✧ Palatial Vanbrugh mansion with a remarkable Great Hall

At Grimsthorpe, 11 miles SE of Grantham; private house, open part year

Grim by name but not by nature. Grimsthorpe is one of the great houses of England. To the approaching visitor, it offers Vanbrugh's last masterpiece, a true northern Blenheim. The rear elevation, however, is wholly different, a delightful jumble of earlier towers, gables and chimney flues, no two bays the same.

The house has belonged to the Willoughby de Eresby family from the 16th century to the present day. Its architectural history reflects their fluctuating fortunes, as variously Barons, Earls and even Dukes (of Ancaster). The original barony was one of the few that could descend through the female line, greatly simplifying the genealogy. The house, now owned by a charitable trust, is occupied by the 27th Baroness Willoughby de Eresby.

Vanbrugh's front elevation, when seen from a distance, seems weak, its recessed centre flanked by pavilions. It might be a child hiding between the skirts of two governesses. Yet the façade grows in potency on closer view, eventually displaying true Vanbrughian energy. The seven centre bays have

houses of England ... a true northern Blenheim.'

uniformly arched windows, framed by paired rusticated columns and a strong entablature. The parapet carries plinths and triumphal statues, glorifying what was the newly ducal house of Willoughby. This is a true architectural calling card.

The Great Hall interior is to Pevsner 'unquestionably Vanbrugh's finest room'. It has the scale of a Tudor great hall but the perspective of a Roman palace. The walls are composed of two storeys of restless arcades, some open, some blind. One upper tier contains grisailles of English kings. The chimneypiece is thought to be by Hawksmoor. The arms are those of George I, who gave Willoughby his dukedom. Behind arched screens on either side of the Great Hall are double flights of stairs, rising theatrically as if the foyers of an opera house. An arched door beneath each landing leads to Vanbrugh's Piranesian undercroft. The doorcases to the floors above are Michelangelesque.

Below The walls of the Great Hall are pierced by arches, some forming doors and windows, others framing works of art. A blind arcade high on the chimney wall contains full-length portraits, painted in grisaille by Sir James Thornhill, of English kings who had seen fit to favour the Willoughby family in the past.

Above The state drawing room was originally the Tudor Presence Chamber and was redecorated by the 3rd Duke of Ancaster in the 1760s, when it served as a dining room. A full-length Reynolds portrait of the Duke is on the south wall. **Right** The King James room takes its name from the portrait of James I that hangs there. The King stayed in the house as a guest of the 14th Baron, later the 1st Earl of Lindsey. The Earl's posthumous portrait hangs above the fireplace.

Some of the upstairs rooms are original to the earlier house, some were inserted by Vanbrugh and some later. The state dining room is original but redecorated and has a Rococo chimneypiece by Henry Cheere. At the end of the room is the Coronation Banquet throne used by George IV, presumably designed to accommodate his girth. The east range contains state rooms inserted in the 18th century, some making use of Tudor oriels, others with new bow windows.

The King James Room has fluted gilt pilasters and a full-length portrait of James I. The state drawing room moves forward to Charles I and his family, in a group of portraits 'derived from' Mytens and van Dyck. The Tapestry Room reverts to the earliest part of the house, with a lower ceiling. The tapestries are from the Soho workshop and the wall mirrors are, for some reason, from the Danieli Hotel in Venice. The diversity of Grimsthorpe's furniture derives from the need to restock it after a disastrous sale of contents in 1828.

Along the back of the central courtyard is a corridor hung with Willoughbys galore. The family served as hereditary Lord Great Chamberlain, the perk taking the strange form of regular gifts of royal chairs, now scattered throughout the house. The Gothic bedroom has a canopy tester from the House of Lords, en suite with the royal throne now in the dining room. The Tapestry Bedroom contains a Gothick bed with crockets climbing the frame like snails.

At the end of the upper corridor is the chapel gallery. Here, almost hidden, is a great treasure, Zurbarán's *Benjamin*, missing from the set now at Bishop Auckland Castle in Durham. Delightful though it is, he seems orphaned from the rest of his family. Some deal could surely be done to make the set complete. The chapel itself is a superlative work, by Vanbrugh or Hawksmoor in full mastery of the classical language. A giant Venetian window lights serene pews and a lofty pulpit.

Next door is the sort of contrast in which English houses excel. Baroque trumpets give way to delicate minuets. The Chinese Drawing Room at Grimsthorpe is one of the finest of the genre. Each ceiling panel carries a different pattern. Yellow and black pilasters frame the Gothick fan vault in the bow window. Lacquered cabinets sit against a wall. The wall-hangings are Chinese paper of delicate trees and fronds against a soft blue background. Coloured birds seem to dance across the walls. This is an exquisite chamber.

Gunby hall

★ ★ ★ A Lincolnshire squire's home with a red-brick William-and-Mary façade

At Gunby, 7 miles W of Skegness; National Trust, open part year

Gunby sits comfortably above a fold in the Wolds. Below lie the flatlands of the Lincolnshire fens, than which nothing is flatter. The house is reputedly Tennyson's model for an English house 'Softer than sleep – all things in order stored,/ A haunt of ancient peace.'

The home of Massingberds since the 15th century, Gunby was threatened by an airfield in the last war. It was saved by the intervention of the owner, Field-Marshal Sir Archibald Montgomery-Massingberd, whose name alone must have daunted the Air Ministry. The house passed to the National Trust in 1944 and is tenanted. Hugh Montgomery-Massingberd's excellent country house books are on display.

'... an Augustan squire's domain, **robust, unostentatious, dignified** and a trifle **prim** ...' – James Lees-Milne

The exterior is a sophisticated William-and-Mary façade of 1700, red brick with stone dressings beneath a severe brick parapet. The interiors are domestic and unspectacular. The drawing room contains portraits by Reynolds of Bennet Langton and his wife, friends of Dr Johnson. Langton so admired Johnson that he would read the latter's dictionary to his family at meals, while his valet combed his hair.

In the ante-room are Victorian watercolours and a model of a Napoleonic battleship. The latter is made of mutton bones gnawed into shape by prisoners of war. The dining room is prettily divided by a screen with barley-sugar balusters. On the wall hangs an Arthur Hughes portrait of Margaret Massingberd in rustic pose with a basket of flowers and doves overhead. The generous staircase has three balusters to each tread and a fine plaster ceiling.

The library was recently restored with a bequest from James Lees-Milne, long a lover of this place. He did more than anyone to ease the passage of fine houses into National Trust ownership in the middle years of the 20th century. His description of Gunby as 'an Augustan squire's domain, robust, unostentatious, dignified and a trifle prim' is the happiest of many in his memoirs.

Harlaxton manor

★★★★ Victorian fantasy mansion with extraordinary interiors

At Harlaxton, 3 miles SW of Grantham; private house, open by arrangement

When Victorian architecture is as valued as Georgian, Harlaxton will be honoured as a masterpiece. Why classical revivalism should be regarded as 'pure' and other revivals as ersatz is a mystery of art history. Either way, the extraordinary Gregory Gregory, builder of Harlaxton, ranks with the Scarisbricks of Lancashire and the Shrewsburys of Staffordshire as English precursors of Ludwig of Bavaria. Gregory's inspiration appears to have been Walter Scott and perhaps Byron.

The house clings to the edge of a hill overlooking the Vale of Belvoir, with the Duke of Rutland's castle in the distance. Gregory was determined to outdo his aristocratic neighbour. Modestly rich, he was born in 1786 and remained a bachelor, devoting his life to researching and building his palace. In 1832, he began work with Anthony Salvin on what was then a purely Elizabethan mansion. Soon afterwards he dispensed with Salvin and hired William Burn, the house interior moving towards Jacobean and, in the astonishing staircase, to Baroque. The reclusive Gregory died in 1854. Although he lived in the house, like many over-ambitious Victorians, he never saw it complete. He designed a family wing but it lay empty. He had a modest staff of only fourteen.

Above The plasterwork decoration of the Cedar Staircase is a triumph of the stuccoist's art. The identity of the stuccoist remains unknown, but the work is usually ascribed to the firm of Bernasconi, who had the skills needed to accomplish such a complex project. An alternative suggestion is that Salvin, after a visit to Bavaria in 1835, imported German craftsmen who were accustomed to the Baroque style and these stuccoists remained after Salvin's departure.

Harlaxton passed through various Gregory descendants until, in 1937, it was on the point of demolition. It was saved by Violet Van der Elst, a remarkable cosmetic tycoon. Offspring of a coal porter and a washerwoman, she invented brushless shaving cream. On the strength of this fortune, she bought Harlaxton, held séances in the library and fought against capital punishment, haranguing crowds outside prisons where they were held. She sold the house to the Jesuits, who passed it to Stanford University and eventually to Indiana's University of Evansville, now its admirable custodian.

The excitement of Harlaxton lies in the interplay of fantasy medieval exterior and eclectic interior. Its silver-gold towers, chimneys and gables rise like a fairy castle at the end of a mile-long drive. Close to, the front is a restless façade of projecting and receding windows, as if Salvin could not bear flatness. The roofline is festooned with scrollwork parapets and stone carvings. Massive lions languish on plinths. Putti grasp at grapes. Walls, pavilions, steps and balustrades are as inventive as in any Austrian belvedere.

Little is known of the genesis of the interiors,
except that Gregory himself played a large part in
their selection. While the dominant style is
Baroque, of the heaviest and most Germanic sort,
diversions are made into Elizabethan, Louis XIV
and Rococo. The quality of recent restoration is
admirable. Stuccowork, gilding, woodwork, even
door-plates are alive and colourful. Only furniture
is missing, a serious loss.

The entrance hall is dominated by a screen as
brutal as a Baroque thug spoiling for a fight.
Rusticated arches rise to an urn and stairs
beyond. They are covered in studs. Baroque
scrolls are hung with curved trophies. The door-
plates are of etched bronze. The stairs rise to the
state dining room with a grand view down the
main drive. Here we are still with Salvin. The
ceiling is in the richest Elizabethan stucco with
heavy pendants, the chimneypiece of stately
marble. The room has the two biggest 'secret
doors' I have seen, taking two men to open them.

Beyond is the Great Hall, with a massive
Jacobean fireplace rising to huge wooden brackets
under the roof. Screen and panels burst with
Mannerist detail. The bay window has heraldic
glass by Willement. The ante-room next door is
a complete contrast. It is serenely Italian, in white
and green, with panels of foxes and pheasants
playing round Rococo trophies. The Long Gallery
fills the east wing of the house. As in the ante-
room, Gregory here used French rather than
English themes. The ceiling is a startling blue sky,
with clouds framed by gilded Rococo panels.
Doorways are of mottled marble.

Beyond is the original conservatory, still moist
and warm, leading appropriately towards the
gardens up the hillside. The last room in this
sequence is the Gold Drawing Room. This might
be an imitation of the Elizabeth Saloon at Belvoir,
wholly French in inspiration with imported
Louis Quinze panels and Rococo doors. A deeply
coved frieze is crammed with putti gazing up to
a ceiling in the style of Tiepolo.

The climax of Harlaxton is now reached, the
Cedar Staircase. This is High Baroque revival,
unique of this style in England. Three tiers of
balconies rise in a series of distorting perspectives
to a billowing *trompe-l'œil* sky. The balconies are
of cedar, the walls of stone, the sculptures of
stucco. The scenery in this stage set is crowded
with putti holding scallop shells, as if Gregory
could not bear to climb upstairs alone. The whole
is 'clothed' in tent-like folds of fake drapery and
tassels. The illusion of movement through space
is enhanced by the inner landing walls being of
mirror glass. Looking down from the topmost
cornice is Father Time wielding a real scythe. He
is attended by a medallion of Gregory himself.

Nobody knows who executed this astonishing
work. The Italian firm of Bernasconi was said to
be the only one in England capable of such
bravura, possibly directed by Burn's assistant,
David Bryce. Like everything at Harlaxton, we
are left mesmerized by Gregory's restless
imagination, his obsession with theatrical effect.

'... we are left **mesmerized** by Gregory's
restless imagination, his obsession
with **theatrical effect.'**

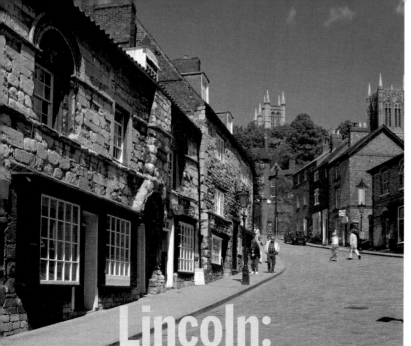

Lincoln: Jew's house

⭐ Ancient house in an ancient street

Steep Hill, Lincoln; now a restaurant

This building, widely proclaimed as the oldest occupied house in England, is one of three Norman survivors on the hill running down from Lincoln Cathedral. The house was built *c*1180 in an area of the city occupied by Jews until the expulsion of 1290. A celebrated Jewish wedding took place here in 1275 when Judith Belaset married Master Benedict, son of Master Moses of the City of London. The house later passed to the Dean and Chapter of Lincoln Cathedral but retained its old association in the name.

The outside is of stone, which must have been luxurious in the 12th-century city. Although later shop fronts have intruded on the ground floor, a round Norman arch below a chimneybreast covers the door and two round arches frame the upstairs windows. That on the left would have lit the hall of the house. That on the right was reputedly for a synagogue, with a courtyard behind. The ensemble is picturesque.

Jew's House is now a restaurant, much used to visitors requesting a look inside. They will see a few Norman arches and an early fireplace.

'The house is a **detective story** of alterations.'

The house has been a seat of Lincolnshire Thorolds since the 1380s. At the time of writing, it is being comprehensively restored by John Thorold as a family home. Fragments of other Thorold houses fill the rooms and are helping to bring to life the old house, long occupied by the renowned topographer, Henry Thorold, but allowed to fall into severe neglect. The rescue is an act of devotion.

The house is a detective story of alterations. There is evidence of an Elizabethan E-plan round a small hall. This

Marston hall

⭐ An Elizabethan house with Georgian additions

At Marston, 6 miles N of Grantham; private house, open part year

was given a floor and then rearranged in the 18th century. The wings and the gatehouse were demolished so we now have only the trunk of a house, with a later extension. Over the porch is a Thorold coat of arms and battered trophy.

Inside, nothing seems to be where it was or should be. The screens passage is a ghost and the hall has been sub-divided. The fireplace, with its magnificent overmantel of caryatids and strapwork, has been moved, perhaps more than once. Panelling, ceilings and windows are now emerging from the partitions of time.

The staircase is lined with Thorold portraits, including a fine Batoni. In an upstairs room is panelling and a jolly ceiling with Baroque shells and Thorold arms. These are dated 1699 and were imported from a previous Thorold house in Devon. Downstairs is some classy, unobtrusive work by the neo-Georgian architect, Francis Johnson. It was only in the 1980s, when a visiting architectural writer described Marston as 'the coldest house in England', that Henry Thorold recognized the suffering of his guests and installed some heating.

Normanby hall

he Sheffield family link to Normanby is strong and much proclaimed. The early Sheffields held numerous properties in the East Midlands. They commissioned Robert Smythson to build what was a magnificent house here on their Lincolnshire estate but the family soon moved on to grander things. By 1703, they were Dukes of Buckingham and later built a mansion in Pimlico that was sold to George III, to become Buckingham (sadly not Sheffield) Palace. Normanby passed to an illegitimate son, reverting to a Sir Robert Sheffield in 1815.

In the 1820s, Sheffield commissioned Robert Smirke to build a house in the prevailing classical style. Despite its isolated location, Normanby became a favourite of his descendants, who extended and modernized it over the years. By the 1940s, it was impossibly big and was partially demolished. In 1963, a younger generation of Sheffields decided to move to Sutton Park, in Yorkshire, instead. Normanby was then leased to the local council and sits today in spacious grounds amid the otherwise scruffy industrial landscape of Humberside.

The exterior is severe. Three fronts of grey ashlar have no decorative adornment, other than columns supporting the porch. The inside was a different matter. Today, the downstairs has been restored to its Smirkean glory. Finest is the entrance hall where today's custodian awaits visitors dressed as a butler, the tickets being sold (on my visit) by a Victorian housekeeper. A classical screen divides the entrance area from what amounts to a drawing room round a fireplace, a pleasantly domestic welcome.

Smirke was a master of planning. The entrance hall turns at right angles into the staircase hall, through another screen of Ionic pillars. The staircase divides into two arms at the window. The composition is overseen by a fine Mytens painting of Charles I. The two chief reception rooms downstairs are the West and East Silk Drawing Rooms, both well restored and full of loudly ticking clocks. Among the family portraits is an infant Sheffield painted shortly after his death. Briefly Marquis of Normanby, his corpse presumably could not be left uncommemorated.

The furniture is of high quality but in these museum settings somewhat cold. The finest piece is a bookcase by Gillow in the library. It has swirling tracery in the glass doors and dominates the books imprisoned inside. Normanby has a fine walled garden.

Spalding: Ayscoughfee hall

⭐ Medieval merchant's house, much added to through the ages

Churchgate, Spalding; museum, open all year

Ayscoughfee is one of those mish-mash houses to be found in most English towns. It has medieval bits and Tudor bits and was then georgianized, gothicized and victorianized. Finally it was stripped, scrubbed, cleaned and enslaved as a museum. All we can do is enjoy the bits that take our fancy.

The original house was built in the 1450s by Richard Alwyn, a Fenland wool merchant. Wool travelling down the River Welland from the interior brought wealth to every community through which it passed. Alwyn's house went to the Ayscoughs, in whose 'fee' it was, and later to the Johnsons. Maurice Johnson founded the Spalding Gentlemen's Society, the oldest antiquarian society in the country, in 1710. The house passed to Spalding Council in 1902 and is now run as a museum of Fenland life.

The form of the house is still essentially late medieval, but the character derives from its gothicization in the 1840s. The exterior was given Victorian windows and gables. The entrance is through a pleasant loggia into the Great Hall. This has been 'Adamized', with a balcony carried on classical pillars. The interior is almost all museum, but includes one delightful room, the old library. This has dark panelled walls and panelled ceiling, with a large arched alcove filled with old leather books. The room forms a vivid contrast with the museum round it, rich, learned and mildly eccentric. Behind it is a vaulted staircase from the medieval house.

Ayscoughfee's prize possession is a glorious yew hedge in the garden. Its eccentric shape seems to have a life of its own, a relief from the adjacent municipalization.

Stoke Rochford hall

★ ★ Victorian mansion built in grand Jacobethan style

At Stoke Rochford, 6 miles S of Grantham; private house, open by arrangement

This is a poor man's Harlaxton, except that it is hardly poor. The seat of the 17th-century Turnor family, whose splendid tombs fill the local church, was rebuilt by Christopher Turnor in 1841. It was in direct emulation of Gregory's Harlaxton. Turnor even went to the same architect, William Burn, and selected a similar site above a steep valley, for similar ostentatious effect. The entrance drive sweeps downhill from the road and up to an obelisk dedicated to Isaac Newton. It then turns to confront the main façade. This approach has been marred by the National Union of Teachers, which runs the house as a residential conference centre and has built a dreadful campus in front.

Turnor did not get another Harlaxton, but he got scale. Stoke Rochford is a gigantic work of Jacobethan revival. It has all the customary signatures – gables, chimneys, towers and projecting wings – adorned with strapwork. They are at their best when seen through a fine set of iron gates. The terrace and view from the far side of the house survives unspoilt.

The interior is mostly intact. The Great Hall retains an arcaded screens passage. Beyond are three gigantic reception rooms looking out over the valley, dining room, drawing room and library; all retain wood-panelled or plaster ceilings. The most distinctive Burn works are the fireplaces. The one in the Oak Room is stupendous, possibly a Flemish 17th-century import and, to Pevsner, 'the most spectacular of its type in England'.

The house was tenanted in the late 19th century but in 1903 another Christopher Turnor inherited it and decided to move in. When he arrived with his wife, the village hung out banners pleading 'Make This Your Home'. He did more than that. He filled the house with villagers, groups, seminars, working men's clubs and 'people of goodwill'. This liberal hospitality continued until the Second World War, when Stoke Rochford became the headquarters of the Parachute Regiment and claimed the planning of the Arnhem raid. Since Moor Park, in Hertfordshire, also claims responsibility, this may explain its disastrous outcome. Turnor himself carved Mediterranean scenes on the staircase. The house then passed into the twilight world of education.

Tattershall castle

'Tattershall ... was **built for show** ... one of the **earliest brick structures** in England.'

☆ ☆ Medieval brick tower, all that remains of a major castle

At Tattershall, 11 miles NW of Boston; National Trust, open part year

In 1911 Lord Curzon discovered that the Fortescues had sold their ancestral pile at Tattershall to speculators. The magnificent 15th-century chimneypieces were already on their way to London Docks for shipping to America. Curzon instantly bought the castle, raced to the Docks and rescued the fireplaces, bequeathing them all to the National Trust in 1925.

Tattershall Castle was built for show and is one of the earliest brick structures in England. Ralph, Lord Cromwell fought at Agincourt in 1415 and became King's Treasurer in 1433, a post with opportunities for personal enrichment that he exploited to the full. He was among the wealthiest men in Henry VI's unhappy kingdom, living and travelling with a retinue of over 100 liveried men, not including servants. Regular decrees were passed forbidding such magnates to bring their retinues to London, but Cromwell was in the habit of going to town with 120 horsemen.

Tattershall Tower was built at the height of Cromwell's wealth. The tower was added to a hall and other buildings of what was already a substantial castle. Brick was newly fashionable and in this material Tattershall was equalled at the time only by Herstmonceux Castle, in Sussex. It is in reality a glorified solar wing, dressed up in military guise. The castle has gone but the tower is still approached across the remains of its moat and outer ward. It stands stark and lonely.

The four storeys of grand rooms are a palace in the sky. The corner turrets were once capped with spirelets. The interiors have no dining room or kitchen, functions performed in the now vanished hall. The building was essential for privacy, each bedroom being surrounded by lesser rooms buried in corner towers and walls. The tower thus has forty-eight distinct chambers, with latrines on each floor. None of the rooms are approached directly from the spiral stairs but always through some device or ante-chamber. The entry to the Audience Chamber on the second floor is in the form of a brick-vaulted passage, virtually a gallery. The chimneypieces have Cromwell's fat purse as emblems.

If Lord Curzon could save and restore the upper storeys and replace the floors, the National Trust could surely refurnish the interiors. Medieval need not mean empty.

Woolsthorpe manor

⭐ Simple farmhouse, famous as the birthplace of Isaac Newton

At Woolsthorpe-by-Colsterworth, 8 miles S of Grantham; National Trust, open part year

Sir Isaac Newton
1642–1727

Isaac's mother was widowed three months before he was born. She remarried when he was three years old, but he remained at Woolsthorpe with his grandmother. He spent his adult life in Cambridge, where he became Lucasian Professor at the age of 27, and in London. He was rewarded with several important government positions in recognition of his scientific achievements.

Isaac Newton was born in the same year, 1642, that Galileo died. He was brought up in a simple cottage south of Lincoln, the son of an illiterate farmer. He left home at twelve and went on to Grantham Grammar School and Cambridge, returning only in 1665 to escape the plague in Cambridge. It is said that it was here that he invented differential calculus and conducted his celebrated experiments with prisms. He must have been inspired by the soft Lincolnshire rain. The house remained a farmhouse but was acquired by the Royal Society in 1942 and opened to the public.

The house is secluded, still with its old farmyard, on a sloping hillside outside the village of Woolsthorpe. Creamy stone walls support a tiled roof. The entrance is reached past a small orchard in which, so legend claims, is a sapling of the apple tree under which the great man sat and felt the force of gravitation. The orchard is unchanged.

The interior of the house could hardly be more simple, nothing but a farmhouse. On the ground floor is the parlour and the kitchen, with 17th-century furniture. There are signs of graffiti said to be those of young Newton unable to find paper and frantically using the walls for his calculations. Experts conclude only that they 'may' have been by Newton.

In the bedroom upstairs is displayed Pope's celebrated epitaph on Newton's birthday: 'Nature and Nature's laws lay hid in night:/ God said, Let Newton Be! and there was light.' The other room is reputedly Newton's study, although he rarely visited in adulthood. In the closet is a reconstruction of his prism experiment.

Rockingham Castle

Northamptonshire

Althorp

'... at Althorp the **family demands attention.**'

Above The picture gallery was created by Robert Spencer, 2nd Earl of Sunderland, on the site of Althorp's former Elizabethan gallery. The Earl had the room repanelled in 1682 as a suitable backdrop for his collection of paintings. Many of the portraits are ladies of Charles II's court who were famed for their beauty, painted by Sir Peter Lely.

★★★★ Elizabethan mansion with Restoration and Georgian alterations

5 miles NW of Northampton; private house, open part year

Which lasts longer, a house or a family? The answer is usually a house. But at Althorp the family demands attention. The childhood home of Diana, Princess of Wales, was turned after her death into a shrine by her brother, the 9th Earl Spencer. An 'event' is staged each year on its annual reopening, as if on a saint's day. The Diana museum is restrained and tasteful.

The Spencers were sheep farmers from Warwickshire when sheep was England's oil. They acquired the estate of Althorp in 1508 and by the end of the century had built the house with courtyard and projecting wings. That plan survives, albeit altered beyond recognition. The exterior was remodelled in the 1660s, when the central court was filled with the present grand staircase.

It was remodelled again in 1787 by Henry Holland for the 2nd Earl Spencer, who amassed at Althorp the greatest private library in the world, including 58 works by Caxton. The new façade was in white brick and mathematical tiling. Unlike English limestone, these materials do not warm with age or sun. To the modern eye, they plead for stucco or the removal of the tiles to reveal the brick beneath. Althorp's exterior is frankly dull. Sacheverell Sitwell remarked that here 'we may feel that architecture is nearly at an end. So little less and it will have gone.'

Interiors were a different matter. The entrance hall is a majestic room, probably designed by Roger Morris by 1733 and rising two storeys to a great coffered ceiling. It is dominated by canvases of Spencers riding to hounds by John Wootton. Even the plasterwork depicts foxes and hounds. The floor is chequerboard. The room evokes the tastes and leisure habits of the landed gentry.

Althorp's furnishings benefited greatly from the family's abandonment in the 20th century of Spencer House in London's Green Park. Downstairs rooms were designed by Holland but remodelled by the ponderous Victorian, J. MacVicar Anderson. The billiard room leads into the library, once one of the finest in private hands in England, now moved to the John Rylands Library in Manchester. Here hangs a Reynolds of a four-year-old Viscount Althorp.

The Restoration staircase at Althorp is a marvellous set piece. It uses the entire two-storeyed saloon as its setting, rising in a single flight to the gallery. It might be the entrance to the grand circle of an opera house, with the picture gallery above as chorus, and van Dyck as soloist.

The saloon walls, below and on the landing above, are hung almost entirely with portraits of Spencers and their relatives. Artists include Kneller, van Loo, Orpen and Augustus John. In pride of place at the head of the landing, the present Earl has shamelessly placed himself and his late sister, Diana, an egotistical gesture of which his Restoration ancestors would have approved.

The picture gallery was converted from that of the Elizabethan house. A collection of Lely 'court beauties' all bear a notable resemblance to Nell Gwynn, but are splendid when shown en masse. At the end of the gallery is van Dyck's *War and Peace*. It shows the two young aristocrats, the 2nd Earl of Bristol and 1st Duke of Bedford, brothers-in-law who were to fight on opposing sides in the Civil War. The painting became a metaphor for the divisions of loyalty caused by that tragic conflict. Bedford, in flaming red attire, looks by far the more 'cavalier' of the two yet he is the one who fought for Parliament.

The stables, flanking the entrance drive, are a superb composition of 1732 by Roger Morris. Their portico is a copy of St Paul's, Covent Garden, by Inigo Jones, to whom the building is a clear act of homage. Homage of a different sort is paid to Diana, Princess of Wales, in the exhibition within.

'The entrance hall ... evokes the **tastes and leisure habits** of the landed gentry.'

★★★★ A French-style palace built onto Elizabethan mansion

3 miles NE of Kettering; private house, open part year

The sight of Boughton across the park from the main road might be of a chateau in the Ile de France. The creamy limestone, the tall first-floor windows, the mansard roof and prominent dormers all speak French. French too is the rusticated entrance loggia. Even the stables look French, as if horses outranked servants. Yet this is a seat of the mighty Dukes of Buccleuch, than which nothing is more English – or Scottish.

The main entrance front of the house was built in the French style by the 1st Duke of Montagu after completing service as British ambassador to the court of Louis XIV in 1678. Any man returning from such a post would have his head abuzz with architecture. Petworth, in Sussex, is of the same period and demonstrates similar influences. Yet Boughton's front is only a front. The house was a Tudor manor set round a series of courtyards that survive behind the 1st Duke's cold Continental façade. They give Boughton a welcome variety.

This is immediately evident when we turn the corner from the main front towards the garden. Here the mood changes. This façade is of refaced Tudor rooms, their roofs betraying various periods of construction. Further to the right is a hinterland of 16th and 17th-century buildings, leading to the

Boughton house

'Boughton's interiors are those of **two houses,** a grand palace ... and [a] more **intimate predecessor.'**

Above The Low Pavilion ante-room was originally the entrance to a group of chambers set aside for important visitors or members of the 1st Duke of Montagu's family. For the last hundred years it has served as an ante-room to the Duke's office. The furniture is Montagu's although the paintings were brought together here by the 9th Duke of Buccleuch.

Georgian dower house. This makes Boughton not so much a house as a hamlet, still set in its park and completely rural. Beyond stretch six avenues of limes and oaks beyond lakes and canals, their formality predating the naturalism of Capability Brown.

Boughton's interiors are those of two houses, a grand palace attached to an earlier and more intimate predecessor. The entrance is attributed to a Frenchman named Pierre Pouget who also worked on Montagu's London house (now the site of the British Museum). Entry is directly up the main staircase from the side of the loggia, another Continental feature. A giant ceiling depicts Discord throwing the Apple amongst the Gods. The balustrade is of iron.

To the right of the stairs are the Low and High Pavilion ante-rooms, containing masterpieces from the extensive Buccleuch art collection. Here hang works by El Greco, Murillo and a portrait of

the 1st Duke by Michael Dahl. The rooms have the demure panelling favoured by the 17th-century Stuart diaspora in France and the Low Countries.

Above the loggia runs Montagu's enfilade of state rooms completed in 1695, a miniature of the enfilade at Hampton Court. Montagu owned the Mortlake tapestry workshop and clearly had the pick of its output. Room after room is hung with the Acts of the Apostles and other biblical themes, interspersed with family portraits by van Dyck and cabinets by Boulle. The final room, formerly the state bedroom, has a nude on the ceiling whose *trompe-l'œil* trick is to rise from her reclining position as the viewer passes beneath her.

Beyond all this lies the earlier house. Directly behind the loggia is the Great Hall, rudely shorn of its entrance status. The 1st Duke 'modernized' the room by inserting a ceiling by the French artist, Louis Chéron. Gainsboroughs adorn the walls beneath more Mortlake tapestries. Gheeraerts depicts Elizabeth I as a mature and stately woman. By the window is an exquisite Boulle 'marriage coffer'.

Left A ceiling painted by Louis Chéron spans the Great Hall. Depicting the apotheosis of Hercules, it was commissioned by Ralph Montagu in 1705, the same year he became the 1st Duke: his ducal coat of arms looks down over the Hall from the western end of the room. **Right** Montagu transformed the Tudor Great Chamber into two smaller rooms, one of which is the Little Hall. He added a gallery in 1694. The ceiling is again by Chéron, this time depicting the return of Prosperine. **Below** The eastern wing of the entrance front was not completed. Instead of the intended suite of grand chambers, it remained an empty shell, but it now houses an interesting miscellany of objects. Chief among these is the Chinese Pavilion shown here, which was made for the 2nd Duke in 1745 and remained in regular use until 1960.

Beyond the Great Hall is the Little Hall, with another Chéron ceiling. This would have been the parlour and family room of the Tudor house. Portraits here are by Kneller, Hogarth and Mengs. A heraldic overmantel depicts the antecedents of the 1st Duke back to the Conquest. Beyond is the drawing room, with an Elizabethan Renaissance fireplace. Its walls are hung with 37 grisailles by van Dyck acquired by the 1st Duke from Lely's estate. They include a rare portrait of van Dyck's contemporary, Rubens.

The rooms now change in key and become more modest, although not in content. The morning room and Rainbow Room continue to prefer Mortlake to wallpaper. In one is a set of Meissen swans made for Madame de Pompadour. Corridors are lined with paintings by Ruisdael, van de Velde and Samuel Scott, looking inwards onto the charming Fish Court of the old Tudor house. They culminate in the old Audit Room, a gallery of Kneller, Lely and Hudson round a long shovelboard table. Against the walls are cases of Sèvres and Meissen.

Boughton goes on and on. Passages and corridors open into halls, armouries and outhouses. This is a true ducal palace. One wing of the new house was never furnished. As if exhausted by the task of filling so much space, the family left it a shell. It now houses a Chinese Pavilion, a picnic tent of brilliant painted oilskin. This looks rather sad in its derelict chamber, as if a garden party had suddenly rushed inside out of the rain. The stables contain the 5th Duke's coach, made in 1830 and painted a magnificent black and yellow.

Below The stable block was added in 1704 as part as Ralph Montagu's expansion at Boughton. On the West front, the building is faced in ashlar stone from nearby Weldon, like the main façade of the house; the East front is red brick.

'Even **the stables** look French, as if **horses outranked servants.'**

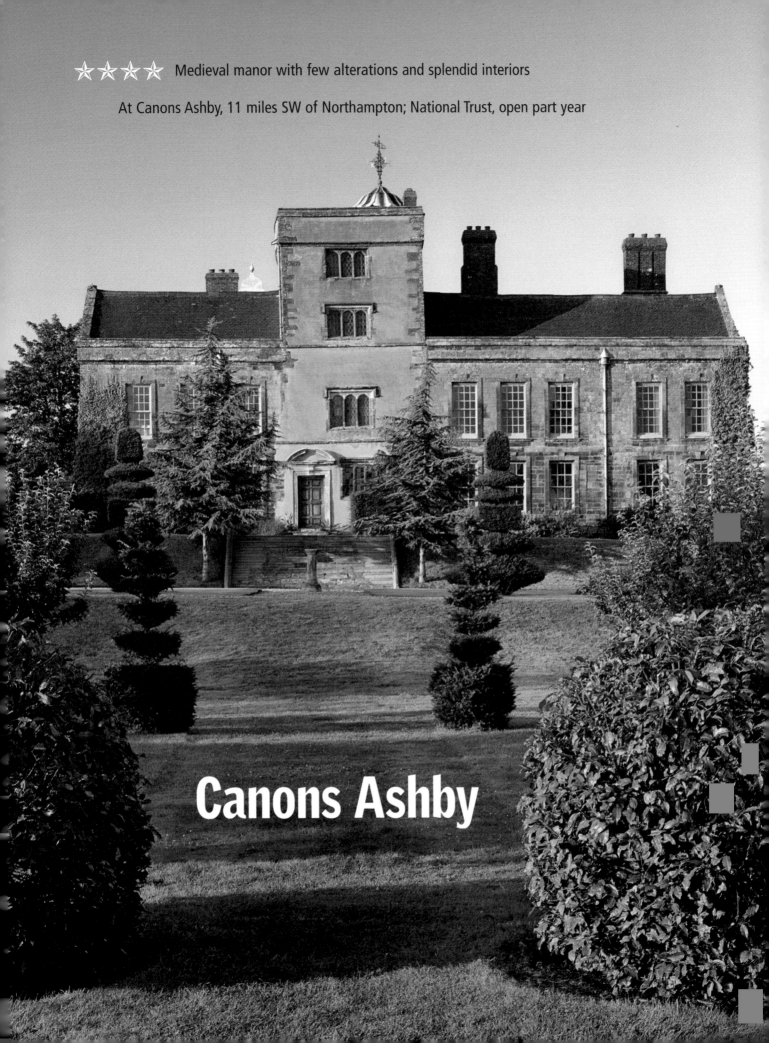

★ ★ ★ ☆ Medieval manor with few alterations and splendid interiors

At Canons Ashby, 11 miles SW of Northampton; National Trust, open part year

Canons Ashby

In 1551, John Dryden married Elizabeth Cope of Canons Ashby, and felt he needed to upgrade the old house to his new status. Yet despite the Drydens' grocery business in London, which later enabled the purchase of a baronetcy, the family were never rich. The new house grew as and when money was available. It was never an aristocratic place, but rather the perfect evocation of a home of the 'middling gentry'. In 1921, *Country Life* described it as 'not calling for admiration ... but quietly compelling it'.

The Drydens became devoted to old Canons Ashby. After a remodelling in the 17th century and, more gently, in the 18th, the house entered a long and merciful slumber. This culminated with Sir Henry Dryden, 'the Antiquary', who lived here from 1818 to 1899 and protected it from all change. Sometimes taken for a tramp, he devoted himself completely to his estate.

The house had no heating or plumbing, just a single tap and a four-seater earth closet in the courtyard. On the birth of his one child, a girl who suffered from polio, he complained that there were already too many women in the house. The daughter became an accomplished photographer.

Queen Mary visited Canons Ashby in 1937 and found it still had neither water nor electricity. Matters then fast degenerated. By 1980 the house was riddled with rot and damp and the garden front threatened to collapse. After a national campaign to raise an endowment, the National Trust accepted ownership and restoration. The remaining Drydens were allocated rooms on the first floor.

The house plan is medieval, grouped round a courtyard of roughly patched stone walls. The entrance is in the courtyard, reached under an arch past the brewhouse. Stone steps rise to a modest door into the Great Hall. This Hall is pleasantly dull, with the customary scatter of antlers and coats of

Left Edward Dryden created the dining room in around 1710. The floor was lowered to improve the room's proportions, the sash windows were inserted and the walls were panelled in oak, with a walnut-framed mirror specially made to fit the overmantel.

Far left At one end of the Elizabethan kitchen is a Victorian range, installed by the National Trust to replace the missing original range. Food would also have been cooked on a stewing hearth, set into a pier between the windows, and in an adjacent bread oven. The high ceilings would have helped to keep temperatures bearable when the kitchen was in full operation.

Below The book room was established by Sir Henry Dryden, 'the Antiquary'. He designed the bookshelves himself and had them built by the estate carpenters in the 1840s and 1850s.

'The panels are covered in leaves, pomegranates and Red Indian princesses ...'

Left The richly carved fireplace and overmantel in the drawing room were commissioned by Sir Erasmus Dryden in the 1590s. The two panels bearing the family coat of arms were added by Edward Dryden in 1710. The brightly coloured decoration was concealed under later stone-coloured paint and was revealed when National Trust conservators stripped the layers away. **Right** In the Tapestry Room, the four-poster bed is flanked by 17th-century Flemish tapestries. The bed is made up of seven 16th-century panels and was assembled by Sir Henry 'the Antiquary' in the 19th century.

arms. The overmantel of war trophies is probably by the 18th-century artist, Elizabeth Creed, an enthusiastic painter of Baroque monuments.

To its right are the service rooms, principally the kitchen and dairy. Next door is a Winter Parlour into which the family would retreat for warmth. Until well into the 1930s, the impecunious Drydens sought to live off whatever the estate could supply, from venison to vegetables. The parlour has walnut panelling of the 1590s, decorated with cartouches of Dryden heraldry beneath pious Puritan mottoes. The room is well stocked with pewter.

On the other side of the Great Hall is the Elizabethan south range. The dining room was repanelled about 1710 and hung with family portraits. Next door is Sir Henry's beloved book room. He refused to call it a library, a term he used for a room from which books were taken elsewhere. This was for books to be read *in situ*. Below the shelves are cupboards for tools, since guests were expected to help in the garden during their visit.

The room leads into the Painted Parlour, decorated in architectural *trompe-l'œil* by Elizabeth Creed and furnished solely and simply with high-backed walnut chairs. For once an empty room is the more serene.

The visitor now ascends the early 17th-century staircase to the jewel of Canons Ashby,

its drawing room. This was added to the original house by Erasmus Dryden in the 1590s, but of this only the elaborate chimneypiece survives. The room was given an astonishing domed ceiling by his son, John, in the 1630s.

So overpowering is the steep coving and giant central pendant of the ceiling that the walls had to be thickened to sustain them. The panels are covered in leaves, pomegranates and Red Indian princesses, a common Elizabethan motif. The pendant is decorated with women in the form of ships' figureheads. The Dryden arms are picked out in vivid colours above the fireplace.

Beyond the drawing room is Spenser's Room, occupied by the poet on his many visits to the house. (The poet, John Dryden, was a cousin of the owners.) On the walls are recently uncovered 16th-century grisaille murals of the Old Testament. They depict the Puritan theme of the perils of worshipping false gods. The Georgian ceiling is of Rococo papier mâché. Back beyond the stairs is the Tapestry Room, reordered in the 18th century. The Flemish hangings have been restored, although a previous tenant used parts of them as bedding for his dogs.

The gardens have been given back their 18th-century formality, with lawns and terraces falling away down the contours to gentle Northamptonshire meadows.

Cottesbrooke hall

⭐⭐⭐ English Baroque house by Smith of Warwick

At Cottesbrooke, 8 miles N of Northampton; private house, open part year

Cottesbrooke is horses. It is home to the kennels of the Pytchley Hunt and home also to the finest collection of equestrian paintings in England. This is hunting county and horse society. It may, as is often claimed, or may not have been the model for Jane Austen's *Mansfield Park*.

Cottesbrooke was begun in 1702 for Sir John Langham by Francis Smith of Warwick. It was aligned on the tower of Brixworth's Saxon church in the distance. The house is now owned by the Macdonald-Buchanan family, who acquired their equestrian pictures over the last century.

I am not normally a fan of horse paintings, but to wander round Cottesbrooke and see these glorious creatures stabled in such stately frames is to be converted. Ferneley, Marshall, Stubbs and Munnings are all present and correct. Few of their subjects ever seem to rear or gallop. They just stand, their decorum fitting their setting.

The exterior of the house is as Smith designed it, a work of stately English Baroque. The façade is chaperoned by a great-aunt of a cedar to its left. The main block is balanced by two pavilions and a linking passage. The house sits in one of the finest gardens in Northamptonshire, with such enticing 'rooms' as the Philosopher's Garden, the Monkey Pond and the Gladiator Garden.

The interior is country-house Georgian, dominated by paintings and porcelain. The decorative scheme is mostly that of Robert Mitchell who redesigned the rooms in an Adam manner in the 1780s. Two corridors, on the ground and first floors, are formed into galleries. The Pine Room was the original hall and contains pre-Mitchell panelling. It has Baroque scroll sconces and the view towards Brixworth. The staircase hall is in blue with the richest of papier mâché Rococo decoration. There is no room on these walls for horse pictures.

The dining room is home to the great Stubbs painting of Gimcrack, identical to one at Newmarket. It is a surreal depiction of sky and heath, as if horses and jockeys were mere extras. The drawing room, in blue with a red Aubusson carpet, is more delicate, with Zoffany and Devis and a Flemish *trompe-l'œil* cabinet.

Left The cantilevered staircase at Cottesbrooke Hall, with its wrought-iron balustrade, was made by William Marshall, a craftsman who worked at Chatsworth in Derbyshire. The Rococo-style mouldings, made from papier mâché, were crafted by John Woolston, whose work can also be seen at nearby Lamport Hall.

Below The gardens were created in the 20th century and were the work of several designers, including Sir Geoffrey Jellicoe, Robert Weir Schultz and Dame Silvia Crowe. On the Statue Walk, a colourful herbaceous border faces a yew hedge, against which are set four 18th-century statues by Peter Scheemakers, made originally for the Temple of Virtue at Stowe.

Deene park

★★★★ A Tudor mansion, added to over the centuries

At Deene, 6 miles NE of Corby; private house, open part year

There is no escaping Lord Cardigan at Deene. The hero of the Charge of the Light Brigade can be imagined leaping on his horse in the courtyard, commanding the great gates to be swung open and trotting out to inspect his private regiment on parade.

He was the only son among seven daughters of the 6th Earl Cardigan and he was spoilt rotten. Yet he was a dashing figure, who charged to what seemed certain death at Balaclava. His survival, as commander, was incredible luck. The house is full of mementoes of Lord Cardigan, including a painting of him describing the charge to Prince Albert and the royal children. Legend has it that Queen Victoria demanded to be removed from the painting when details of Cardigan's colourful private life later emerged.

The details concerned one Adeline Horsey de Horsey. After serving as Cardigan's longstanding mistress, she and he married secretly in Gibraltar two months after the first Lady Cardigan's death in 1858. Society was scandalized. The couple were twenty-seven years apart in age but were happy throughout their marriage. After Cardigan's death, Adeline flirted with Disraeli, briefly married a Portuguese count, travelled widely, hunted and lived at Deene until her death in 1915. Towards the end of her life she wore thick make-up and a blonde wig, and dressed in her husband's Light Brigade uniform. Her shocking and inaccurate *Recollections* are said to be irresistible.

'The house is as **flamboyant as the family** that has occupied it for almost **500 years.'**

Above The Octagon is a small sitting room, positioned in one of the turrets of the south range of the Tudor part of the house. Three *trompe l'œil* paintings by a 17th-century Flemish artist, Cornelis Gysbrechts, hang on the walls, along with small monochrome portraits of Deene's longest-serving members of staff, painted by Richard Foster in 1970.

The house is as flamboyant as the family that has occupied it for almost 500 years. Its origins are 14th century, fragments of which survive in the inner court. Mostly this is a mansion of *c*1570. The gatehouse gives onto an enclosed court at the far side of which is the Great Hall, with a Renaissance porch and classical frieze.

Inside, the Great Hall has chestnut hammerbeams with carved pendants. The dais end forms a family reredos. Heraldic stained glass in the windows honours the Cardigan family, the Brudenells, and their spouses down the ages. This glass was inconsiderately damaged by an American bomber crashing nearby during the Second World War but is restored. Brudenells gaze down from all sides. Beyond in the billiard room are fragments of the earlier Great Hall.

> '... a house of **passages** and **alcoves**, **treasures** and **surprises**.'

Above The tapestry room was once lined with the hangings that give the room its name, but most were sold in the 1920s and now only one remains. It depicts Joseph receiving his brothers and was made in Brussels some time before 1629.
Above right The Great Hall was enlarged to its present size in the 1570s by Sir Edmund Brudenell. His nephew, Sir Thomas Brudenell, who later became the 1st Earl of Cardigan, added the stained glass windows early in the 17th century. The windows feature the arms of the Brudenells and the families to whom they were related.

Deene is a house of passages and alcoves, treasures and surprises. From the outside it is a mixture of façades, some united by Victorian battlements and neo-Tudor windows. Inside, Jacobean merges into Georgian into Victorian in a decorative continuum. The Oak Staircase with pierced panels in its balustrade leads to a landing overlooking the chapel. This must be the jolliest private chapel in England, with crimson walls and cushions. The old Great Chamber is now a tapestry room. Its late-Elizabethan ceiling is taken from Serlio, a rich swirl of patterns as if made of icing sugar.

A series of restored Elizabethan chambers faces out over the garden. King Henry VII's Room reputedly recalls a visit from that monarch to the earlier house. Sir Edmund's Room has exposed timber and plaster walls, while a sitting room is filled with charming monochrome portraits of staff on the estate.

Grander chambers were added in the 18th and 19th centuries. The Bow Room contains books from a 17th-century Lord Cardigan's library, a Reynolds of the 4th Earl's wife and a fine Gainsborough. Over the dining room fireplace is a dramatic depiction of the 7th Earl leading the famous Charge. What is left of his horse, now just the head, is displayed in the White Hall.

Fawsley hall

⭐ Restored Tudor house in deer park, with a Victorian wing by Salvin

4 miles S of Daventry; now a hotel

Fawsley is a battle-scarred survivor of the 20th century's country-house wars, now put out to grass. It sits in a wide deer park, surrounded by a lake, woods and deferential ducks. The house looks and mostly is Elizabethan. The land belonged to the Knightleys from the early 16th century, they having prospered as promoters of sheep farming in Staffordshire. They cleared two ancient villages at Fawsley to make way for a sheep run.

Knightleys entertained Elizabeth I and sided with Cromwell. In the 18th century they began rebuilding their medieval house but not drastically. In 1869 Anthony Salvin added a wing. The last Lady Knightley befriended John Merrick, the deformed 'Elephant Man', and gave him a cottage on the estate. She died in 1913.

Disaster ensued for Fawsley. The house was occupied by the Ministry of Defence, worst wrecker of country houses since Cromwell. The house did not recover. It became a timber works in the 1960s and, when Pevsner visited it in 1972, was derelict. New money then came over the horizon. The Saunders family bought the old place and restored it as a hotel. Today, it is again a grand house, quietly awaiting guests each weekend. The butler receives visitors at the door, including any just wanting to see round.

Fawsley's pride is still its Great Hall of 1537. This is a huge room with a dramatic projecting bay window. The roof had been removed in the 1960s but has since been reinstated on the basis of a few surviving beams and illustrations. The bay has a fan vault and secret room above it. The shield in the hall has the 334 quarterings of Knightley marriages over the centuries. The medieval wing and courtyard are now the bar and restaurant. The Salvin wing with its Gothic gables and finials contains the main reception rooms. A fire blazes in the fireplace. This is a happy restoration.

Holdenby house

⭐ ⭐ Elizabethan-revival mansion built on the remains of an Elizabethan house

At Holdenby, 6 miles NW of Northampton; private house, open part year

Holdenby was begun in 1571 by Sir Christopher Hatton, local man and glamorous Elizabethan courtier. Born in 1540, he was a 'gentleman pensioner' at twenty-four, vice-chamberlain at thirty-seven and Lord Chancellor at forty-seven. His nickname was 'the dancing chancellor'. Witty, clever and arrogant, he evicted the Bishops of Ely from their London palace, Ely Place, and gave his name to Hatton Garden behind.

In Northamptonshire, Hatton built what was in its day one of the largest houses in England, intended to entertain and impress his Queen. He was explicit, remarking in 1580 that he meant to leave this 'shrine, I mean Holdenby, still unseen until that holy saint may sit in it, to whom it is dedicated'.

She never came. But others arrived to marvel at the place and be entertained by Hatton's agents. Hatton died in 1591, in debt and dismissed as 'a vegetable of the court that sprung up at night and sank again at his noon'. The giant house was used as a prison for Charles I after the Civil War and was then mostly demolished for its stone.

What we see today is what took its place in 1873 at the height of the Elizabethan revival. The new owners, Lord and Lady Clifden, created a long entrance range with an Elizabethan porch, pedimented dormer windows and tall chimneys, all in grey-gold local stone. The windows are stone mullioned and the chimneys capped by odd classical entablatures. The building incorporates Hatton's surviving kitchen wing. The old gate arches stand like silent sentinels in the gardens. Clifden descendants, the Lowthers, still occupy the house.

The interiors are solid Elizabethan revival. A comfortable panelled entrance hall is dominated by a portrait of Louis III of France. The old billiard room is a music museum. Apart from keyboard instruments, it displays such curios as a rain stick and a didgeridoo. The more obviously Victorian dining room has silk wall-hangings and sombre portraits of Stuart courtiers and racehorses. Today the grounds are being restored as a Tudor garden with antique names and Rosemary Verey's 'too-too fragrant border'.

Kelmarsh hall

★ ★ Palladian house designed by James Gibbs and built by Smith of Warwick

At Kelmarsh, 5 miles S of Market Harborough; private house, open part year

Left The staircase hall at Kelmarsh is decorated in a restrained style. Nancy Lancaster was respectful of the original interiors; it was important, she believed, to have 'a feel for a house's personality and try not to fight against it'.

Kelmarsh was bought by a Wigan tycoon, George Lancaster, in 1902 and twenty-six years later it was leased to an upwardly mobile American couple, Ronald and Nancy Tree. Ronald had become the first American Master of the Pytchley Hunt and used this eminence to secure the local seat in Parliament. The Trees then moved to Ditchley, in Oxfordshire, but separated in 1947. Nancy returned to marry George's son and her former landlord at Kelmarsh, Claude Lancaster. She imported the young John Fowler as decorator and the present house is very much their creation. Claude's sister lived at Kelmarsh until it passed to a trust committed to its preservation.

The house is in something of a limbo. It was built by Smith of Warwick to a Palladian design by James Gibbs *c*1730–6. It has no portico, just a brick pediment. The outside is serene and symmetrical, overlooking gardens laid out in part by Geoffrey Jellicoe. The interior was fitted out by Smith, with plasterwork by the Artaris, and later by James Wyatt. Its glory is Smith's hall. This has plasterwork in full 1730s flow, with flowers above the doors and a balcony over a colonnade. The Victorians filled it with antlers and 22 pieces of oriental armour. It is now rather bare.

Behind the hall is the saloon, later in style and possibly by James Wyatt. Here the plaster is more restrained and Adamish, the colour a mid-Georgian blue. Most of the remaining reception rooms are in John Fowler's post-war 'Country House' style, of strong colours and sedate furnishings. The dining room contains American chairs, with handles on their backs presumably for helping ladies to sit down. The Chinese Room has 18th-century wallpaper depicting not just landscape and flora but people and animals, a rarity. In the corridor is a map of the Pytchley country.

Nancy Lancaster liked to fill the hall 'with the three things that were essential to me in any room; real candlelight, wood fires and lovely flowers'. All are needed.

Kirby hall

'Kirby remains **an important work of architecture.**'

⋆ ⋆ Remains of a once-mighty Elizabethan house

Near Deene, 4 miles NE of Corby; English Heritage, open all year

Kirby, like Holdenby (see page 85), belonged to Sir Christopher Hatton. It was begun in 1570 for Sir Humphrey Stafford, Sheriff of Northamptonshire, but on his death five years later was sold to Hatton, whose Holdenby was not yet ready to receive his 'holy saint', should she grace him with a visit. Hatton worked on Kirby alongside Holdenby, as if to offer the Queen which ever was ready first.

She visited neither. James I came to Kirby four times, to visit a distant relative of Hatton's who inherited the house. The state rooms were opened only for that purpose. England was dotted with these royal suites, maintained at vast expense. By 1654, John Evelyn was already finding Kirby a 'seat naked'.

Sales of contents were held in 1772 and again in 1824, by when it was 'going fast to decay'. Estate staff were living in its rooms: a labourer in the library and dogs in the drawing rooms. Stucco ceilings were yielding to 'the vampire ivy'. A Victorian owner, the Earl of Winchelsea, preserved the ruins as picturesque but they passed to the government in 1930, a shepherd being left as custodian.

By the time money was available for restoration, the philosophy was 'conserve as found'. Today, Kirby is part ruin but with its main rooms reinserted. The place seems cold and loveless. Nowhere does the word nationalization stick so emphatically to a building, as if house and park had been weeded, gravelled, manicured and rendered fit for regimental inspection.

Above The loggia was built by a local mason, Thomas Thorpe, in the 1570s and refashioned by Nicholas Stone in the 1630s. Below A view from one of the ground-floor bed chambers, looking south. Sharing the same bay on the first floor is the Great Withdrawing Chamber.

Nonetheless, Kirby remains an important work of architecture. The plan of the house is traditional Elizabethan, a forecourt, gateway and inner Great Court, with its hall lying on the far side. The state rooms lead off the family chambers to the right. Outstanding is the frontispiece of the entrance façade. This was built by Nicholas Stone in the 1630s, apparently as a homage to his master, Inigo Jones. This homage is repeated on the reverse side of the façade in the courtyard. Here giant pilasters rise above a loggia with a central window and balcony, like a house in Paris. Yet when this was erected, Kirby's greatness was already past.

On the far side of the Great Court, Hatton's old house remains. The façade here is transitional, a medieval plan of hall and service rooms, yet symmetrical in outward appearance and covered in Renaissance ornament. The porch, with a window later inserted by Stone, is of the 1570s. It is an English Renaissance masterpiece with three storeys of pilasters, the uppermost with seven attached columns beneath a sumptuous Dutch gable.

The interiors are either ruined or dull. Hall, gallery, Great Chamber and subsidiary rooms were refurnished for the filming of *Mansfield Park*, but then sadly emptied again. The guidebook can only resort to artists' impressions and pictures of other houses of the period. The finest rooms, the Great Withdrawing Chamber and Best Bedchamber, were those used by James I. They have superb bow windows looking out over the gardens. Sitwell described them as 'like two huge galleons tied up at anchor ... the poops of two stone ships, never meant to sail, but only to catch the sunlight'. But he saw them in a sea of glorious weeds.

The grounds have been excavated, restored and replanted in their original parterres. This has been well done. A History in Action festival takes place here each year, with jousting, quaffing, wenching and other adventures. If such 'reinstatement' is allowed in the grounds outside, why not inside? Kirby would have more life as a luxury hotel.

Lamport hall

 House developed from a Tudor manor, with classical frontage begun by
John Webb and completed by Smith of Warwick

Near Lamport, 8 miles N of Northampton; private house, open part year

Sir Gyles Isham, 12th baronet and Hollywood actor (opposite Garbo in *Anna Karenina*), died a
bachelor in 1976. The fate of the house occupied by Ishams since the 16th century was suddenly
in doubt. It was 'not good enough' for the National Trust but ideal for dry rot. The prospect was for a
hotel, flats, conference centre, county museum or miserable decay. Thanks to tax reform, a sort of
salvation has arrived. The house passed to trustees, as Sir Gyles hoped, and a new generation has
been given the task of keeping the place together.

Lamport Hall stands on a hill with cypresses joining more wayward cedars in keeping guard. The
oddest feature of the exterior is a portico trying to show its face above the parapet of the garden
front, not what Francis Smith had in mind in his original design. Beneath is the motto of every great
house, 'In things transitory resteth no glory'.

The villa-like extension was built in 1655 for Sir Justinian Isham by John Webb, pupil of Inigo
Jones. It was just five bays wide and sits in the middle of the present garden front. Inside was to be a
'high Roome' in which Isham intended to receives *des personnes d'honneur*. In the 18th century, this
villa was flanked by longer wings by the Smiths, beginning in 1732. Later generations added fronts to
other sides, greatly extending the size of the house and the burden on the present trustees.

The interior is laid out round the High Room. This is half a cube but with only the mantelpiece
and doorways still by Webb. It is a fine work with heavy swags and broken pediment. Two delightful
swans, the Isham crest, are in attendance. The upper walls are of the Smith period, a century later.
Cameos of kings fill the panels beneath the coving.

The library is a warm, pleasant room filled with Regency bookshelves topped by busts of
worthies. The Oak Room next door, part of the Webb house, has been re-panelled in the Jacobean

style and filled with pewter. Behind is a graceful Georgian staircase brought here in the 19th century. Its delicate 18th-century balusters give way to much heavier Webb ones on the landing above.

Beyond in the China Passage is England's first garden gnome, imported from Nuremberg by the Victorian Sir Charles Isham. These gnomes were originally carried as good luck tokens by German miners. Isham used them to hold place names at table, but later populated his garden with them. Few country house fads have proved so influential. Copies are available in the shop.

The Cabinet Room beyond, once used as a chapel, has the finest Lamport pictures, including works by Sebastiano Ricci, Reni and van Dyck, as well as Italian and Flemish cabinets. But why no video of Gyles Isham's performance with Garbo?

Below left John Webb designed the High Room in 1655 for Sir Justinian Isham, the 2nd Baronet. It was the 6th Baronet, Sir Edmund, who commissioned the ceiling from William Smith in 1740. The plasterwork was executed by local craftsman, John Woolston. **Below right** Webb intended the Oak Room to be an ante-room to the High Room. The panelling is 17th century but was installed in 1907; it is believed to have come from a now-lost house, Great Bayhall in Kent.

Lyveden New Bield

⭐ Unfinished Elizabethan mansion and monument to faith

Near Brigstock, 8 miles NE of Kettering; National Trust, open part year

Tudor England seems so familiar that we easily forget the outlook and loyalties of people still within living memory of the Middle Ages. The Henrician Reformation divided England into the Old and New Religions and his daughter, Mary I, came close to delivering it to Spain. Until the Toleration Acts of the 1680s, counties divided and families fought.

The two great dynasties of Northamptonshire were the Ishams (of Lamport) and the Treshams. Sir Thomas Tresham was born a Protestant, succeeded to his inheritance in 1559 and was knighted by Elizabeth I at Kenilworth. Twenty years later, he met the charismatic Jesuit, Robert Parsons, and became a Roman Catholic. The remainder of his life was spent in and out of prison, however much he protested his loyalty to the Crown and vowed to fight for Elizabeth should 'the Spaniard' land.

Tresham sought to express his faith in more than just his church. He expressed it in domestic architecture. At Lyveden and Rushton (page 97), he created icons in stone. Lyveden, built towards the end of his life, was ostensibly a hunting and banqueting lodge. It was unfinished at his death in 1605 and remains unfinished today.

New Bield is distinct from Sir Thomas's former house at the foot of the slope. It stands isolated on a hill well away from a side road, looking as if a storm has sliced off its roof. The plan is that of a Greek cross. Two wings have large bay windows in the contemporary Elizabethan style. Although the house is open to the sky, the rooms are clearly delineated, with a Great Hall and Great Chamber in one wing and kitchens in another. Near the kitchens are bread ovens and an alcove for a boiler. There are parlours and bedrooms. The house was planned to have another storey, with a lantern giving a panorama over the surrounding Tresham land.

The outer walls are coated with religious symbolism, the emblems of Christ's Passion beautifully cut into stone panels and set in a landscape of mounds, canals and vistas. Here are the purse, torch, spear, sword, cross, ladder, hammer, nails, garment, dice, scourge and crowing cock. Round the basement are shields for Tresham's own heraldry, never carved. They form a melancholic parade of weepers round this strange folly. The formal gardens running down the hill to the Old Bield are now emerging, a most exciting work of garden archaeology.

Nassington: **Prebendal** manor house

★ Medieval hall with even older origins

At Nassington, 7 miles S of Stamford; private house, open part year

Where would England's old houses be without the toil, sweat and tears of the saints who care for them? The Prebendal Manor House at Nassington has been nursed back to life by the present owner, Jane Baile, with a tithe barn and medieval garden by way of support.

The house is old indeed. It is claimed as the site of one of King Canute's manors and to have been visited by him in person. The Great Hall may well be 13th century, with round-arched doors to the screens passage. Two Perpendicular Gothic windows have been reinstated in one wall and large, later, fireplaces opened up. A flue rises impressively to the open-timbered roof. The Hall bay window is buried by later building but, apart from this offence, a modern mezzanine leaves most of the structure open to view. A framed copy of *The Times* for 1966, the last with advertisements on the front page, hangs on the wall, looking almost as ancient as an adjacent patch of wall-painting.

Across from the house are a dovecote and the barn. Nassington is still private. I find these informal custodians of the past preferable to the stripped-down whitewash jobs of the state sector.

Northampton: Abington park

★ Tudor house, with later façade reputedly by Smith of Warwick

Park Avenue South, Northampton; museum, open all year

There are few sadder sights than a historic house trapped by suburbia, like a vintage Rolls stuck in a bypass traffic jam. Abington, with its Shakespeare association, has only its old park to guard its dignity. It is home to yet another didactic lifestyle museum aimed at local primary schools.

The house belonged to a family of London merchants named Bernard, who rebuilt it at the end of the 15th century. To this house came Elizabeth Nash in 1649 to marry John Bernard. She was the widowed grand-daughter of William Shakespeare (see Stratford-upon-Avon: Nash's House, page 178) and his sole executor. Rumours abounded of papers and lost plays hidden about the house. The entrance façade was remodelled, reputedly by Smith of Warwick, between 1738 and 1743 in a rich Northamptonshire ironstone.

The Great Hall is medieval but has replacement hammerbeams. The panelling in the adjacent Oak Room was moved there from the Hall and is excellent, with delicate linenfold sections from floor to ceiling. This room has a 17th-century refectory table, benches, carpet and a dresser. A Tudor staircase appears to have been brought from elsewhere.

Rockingham castle

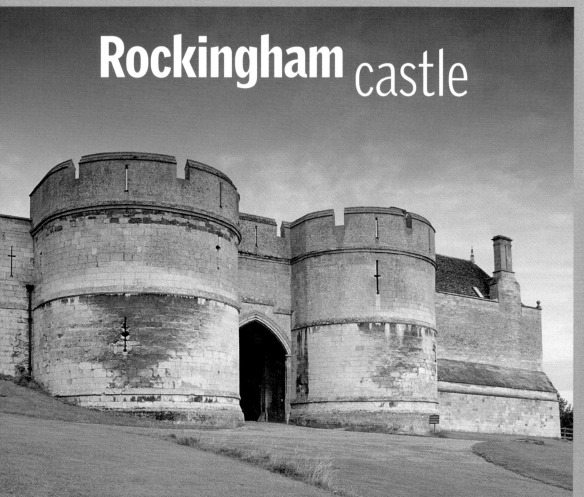

★★☆ Medieval castle with Norman origins and Victorian additions by Salvin

At Rockingham, 1 mile NW of Corby; private house, open part year

Rockingham Castle dances on its bluff over the River Welland, protesting the horrors of Corby to its rear. A castle has stood here since the dawn of history. When no longer serving a military purpose, it was adapted as a home by generations of Watsons. The subsequent house displays the English genius for marrying history to convenience.

The old castle, a royal residence fallen to ruin, was acquired from the Crown by Edward Watson in 1544. It has remained in the same family ever since. Watsons rose to be Earls then Marquesses of Rockingham, allied by marriage to Rutlands, Straffords, Monsons and Sondes. The castle passed through daughters, younger sons and nephews to the present Saunders family. They added the name of Watson as a badge of pride in the castle's custodianship.

Behind its massive gatehouse, Rockingham has the familiar medieval form of a hall with outbuildings within the bailey of an old Norman keep. The Tudors divided the hall both vertically and horizontally and built wings on both ends to form an H-plan. The house remained thus until the 19th century when Anthony Salvin was asked to extend it and revive its medieval past. He crenellated the old

'This is a remarkable **relic** of **medieval** **self-sufficiency.'**

gatehouse, put a flag tower on the façade, cleared up the service wings and built a new residential tower to the rear. As usual with Salvin, the work was deferential and sensitive.

The castle is entered through the gatehouse in the old wall, an approach much loved by film producers. An inner courtyard looks over the Welland Valley towards Leicestershire. The house lies to the left, the gap between it and the old curtain

Left The Street in the castle leads up to the laundry, built 1663–69; the buildings on the right, built c1550, house the kitchen, brewhouse and bakehouse, with the dairy and game larder on the left. The servants quarters were above the kitchen range. **Below** In the Great Hall, the beams with their improving religious texts are dated 1579. The bows displayed above the Tudor fireplace are stone bows, a type of cross bow used for sport that fires stones rather than bolts.

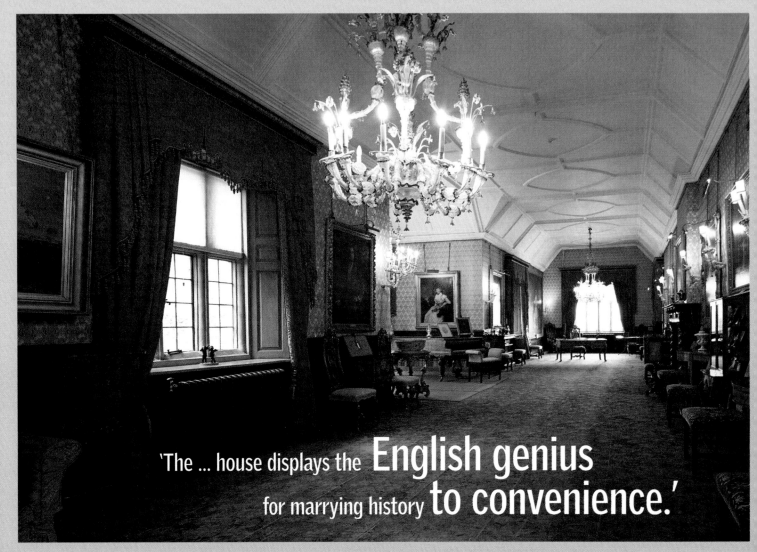

'The ... house displays the **English genius** for marrying history **to convenience.**'

Above The Long Gallery is one third of its original size; slighted during the Civil War by Royalist troops, the damaged end was abandoned when the castle was rebuilt. The deep alcove, housing the piano, was inserted in the 19th century when Anthony Salvin added the flag tower to Rockingham's façade.

wall being filled with outbuildings forming what is called 'The Street'. At its top is a gabled laundry near the old keep. In The Street were the bakehouse, brewery, larders and dairies, with scullery and kitchen adjacent to the old hall. This is a remarkable relic of medieval self-sufficiency.

The present subdivided Great Hall is pleasantly domestic but still has the fireplace of the larger hall. On a beam is the Tudor inscription: 'The howse shal be preserved and never will decaye wheare the almightie God is honored and served daye by daye'. The lobby and staircase are Salvin insertions. Beyond is the Panel Room, with coats of arms of families joined with Watsons. This room, like many in the castle, contains 20th-century paintings collected by the present owner's forebear, Sir Michael Culme-Seymour. They include works by Augustus John, Spencer, Sickert and Hepworth.

The Tudor wing occupies the right-hand side of the courtyard. The Long Gallery contains family portraits by Reynolds and van Dyck and a Zoffany of the Sondes children playing cricket. At one end is a picture by Ben Marshall of brothers out hunting. Rockingham is one of many houses claiming inspiration for Dickens's Chesney Wold in *Bleak House*. The author visited the house at the time and the Armoury in the flag tower is duly named 'Mr Tulkinghorn's Chamber'.

The gardens are dominated by the yew walk, shaped like a herd of elephants about to stampede across the lawn. This hedge is the most warlike feature of modern Rockingham.

Rushton Triangular lodge

★ ★   Religious symbolism wrought in stone

Near Rushton, 3½ miles NW of Kettering; English Heritage, open part year

To call the Triangular Lodge a folly might seem disrespectful of Sir Thomas Tresham's religious belief. His story is told above, under Lyveden New Bield (see page 91). Whereas Lyveden depicts a Greek Cross and is decorated with the Instruments of the Passion, the lodge represents the Trinity of biblical witnesses, the Father, the Word (or the Son) and the Holy Ghost. It also embraces numerous puns on Tresham's name. It is three-sided, three-storeyed, with three bays and three gables to each side, each being 33⅓ feet long. The windows are trefoils, filled with triangular tracery. The chimney is triangular. Even Tresham's wife entered into the trinitarian spirit, calling him 'Good Tres'.

The building was completed in 1597 and is adorned with symbols of the Trinity. Mottoes and texts were painstakingly worked out by Tresham during his period in prison. They have been the subject of laborious analysis (in the guidebook) and form a creed in stone. For all that, the building can be appreciated as a delightful structure built for a purpose, albeit later inhabited by the estate warriner or rabbit breeder. Rabbits, like doves, were protected game for manorial lords, to the fury of their tenants.

The interior comprises three storeys of hexagonal rooms, the corner triangles containing a stair, a chimney and a recess. The windows are small and dark. The house stands in a small enclosure near the main road, guarded by evergreens and looking out over fields and hedges.

Southwick hall

★★ A medieval house with a Georgian wing

At Southwick, 9 miles S of Stamford; private house, open part year

The medieval house was built by the Knyvetts, one of whom was Lord Chancellor to Edward III. It has been restored by the Caprons, one of whom was a BBC editor, which brings things a sort of full circle. It was to Southwick that the BBC brought Alexander Solzhenitsyn in total secrecy for interview after he had left Russia. The house is suitably isolated on the steppes of Rockingham Forest.

Two towers of an old 14th-century house survive at either end of an Elizabethan hall, with an 18th-century extension to one side. The entrance is into one of the towers, a rib-vaulted undercroft which was beneath what was probably the chapel. This appears to have been an addition of c1320 to an earlier hall house, forming a curious and picturesque accumulation of ancient rooms. The Great Hall became a drawing room in the 16th century, its Tudor fireplace still in place.

The most entertaining part of the house is the unaltered medieval chambers upstairs. These include a priest's room of the 1350s and a Gothic room which may have been the chapel. Two old bedrooms inserted above the original hall have unusual barrel roofs, one of them with fine panelling.

A member of the estate staff has collected tools and implements found over the years on the estate, and displayed them in one of the barns. This is a true manorial museum.

Stoke park

Above and right The west pavilion at Stoke Park was once a library. Towards the end of the 18th century it was converted into a ballroom, with a floor-length Venetian window looking out over the terrace.

 Surviving early Palladian pavilions

Near Stoke Bruerne, 7 miles S of Northampton; private house, open part year

The great house was reputedly the first Palladian mansion to be built in England, in 1629 for Sir Francis Crane, director of the famous Mortlake Tapestry Works. The mansion is no more, but its pavilions survive as eerie architectural icons. Like the house to which they were linked by a quadrant colonnade, they are in the early classical style already seen at the Whitehall Banqueting House and the Queen's House in Greenwich. Although the designs were said to have been brought by Crane from Italy, Inigo Jones is generally associated with the project. Either way, two classical pavilions of such an early date merit attention, even if the main house was burned down in 1886. The neo-Jacobean house which replaced it has also gone, replaced by a farmhouse. Stoke is now a place of ghosts, terraces, choked ponds and empty colonnades – and two proud pavilions.

The pavilions have been restored using a bold local ironstone for their giant pilasters. This makes them colourful, almost jazzy. Each is one and a half storeys high with a three-bay façade to the front and a side projection to pick up the surviving colonnades. Such a plan, borrowed from Palladio, was unknown in England at this early date. The hipped roofs are later, as is the Venetian window in the left-hand pavilion, as seen from the park. Both look out over a Victorian terrace flanking a small lake.

The right-hand pavilion was originally the chapel of the big house and is now a private house but the left-hand one, formerly the library, became a ballroom and is accessible to the public. At the end of a mile-long drive from the main road, these stranded monuments have an Ozymandias splendour.

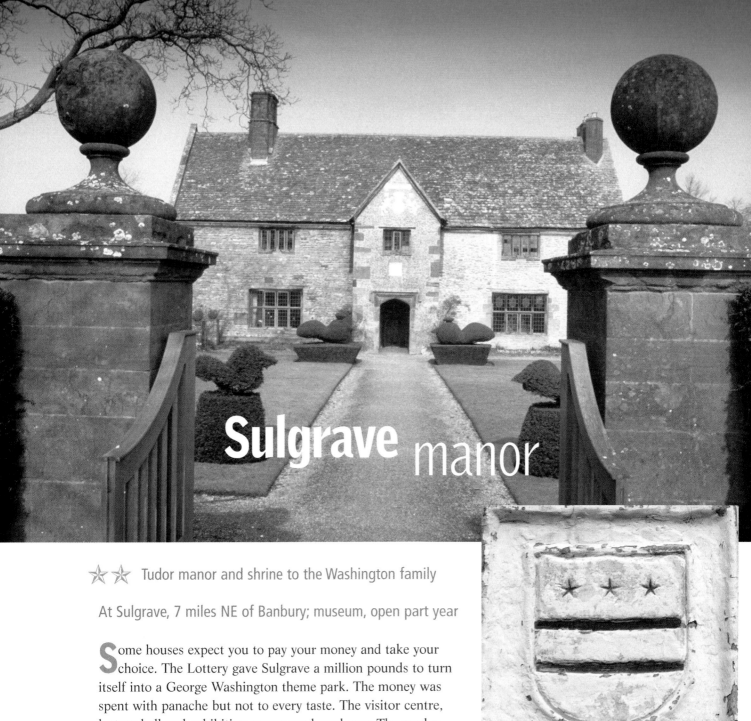

Sulgrave manor

⭐⭐ Tudor manor and shrine to the Washington family

At Sulgrave, 7 miles NE of Banbury; museum, open part year

Some houses expect you to pay your money and take your choice. The Lottery gave Sulgrave a million pounds to turn itself into a George Washington theme park. The money was spent with panache but not to every taste. The visitor centre, lecture hall and exhibition rooms are brand new. The garden is immaculate and actors in Tudor dress say things like, 'Pray come hither, sire', and 'Enter not'. Americans love it.

Sulgrave was the Tudor manor house built by the Washington family of Durham in the 16th century and vacated by them in 1610. This was some time before the birth of John Washington, who emigrated to Virginia in 1656 and was great-grandfather of the first president. But the name is the thing. We could be forgiven for thinking that George himself drank ale by the smoking kitchen fire and galloped his horse across the lawn. When the last owners sold the house in 1914, money was raised for its restoration as a museum, with considerable help from the Colonial Dames of America.

The house is a simple Tudor hall house, restored with great attention to authenticity. The apparent symmetry is deceptive, since the left-hand side of the main porch was rebuilt in the 1920s and the rear wing in the 18th century. Nonetheless, Elizabethan coats of arms crown the porch itself and the old Great Hall remains. The rooms all contain Elizabethan furnishings and paraphernalia. In the

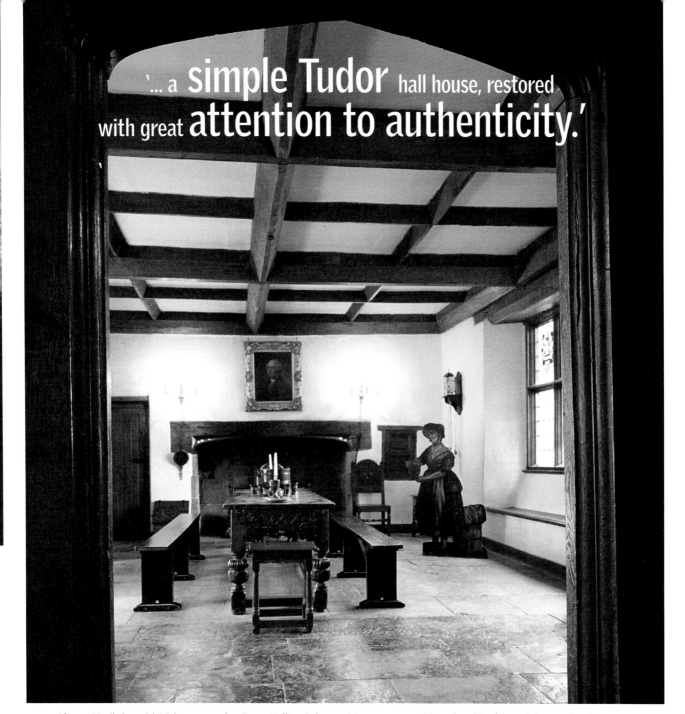

'... a **simple Tudor** hall house, restored with great **attention to authenticity.'**

Above Until the mid 19th century the Great Hall at Sulgrave Manor was partitioned and its fine oak beamed ceiling concealed beneath plaster. Restoration opened the room up again and revealed the Tudor fireplace, with separate salt cupboard to one side. **Left** Above the porch is a relief plaque of the Washington family coat of arms; it has often been claimed that its three stars and two bars influenced the design of the American flag.

window glass is depicted the stars and stripes of the Washington arms (unrelated to the American flag). There are actors in each room – including a lady writing a letter with a quill pen in the Hall.

The 18th-century wing running at right angles to the Hall begins with the Oak Parlour, clad in panelling of about 1700. The kitchen has been furnished from an old manor in Hampshire. On my visit it was in use by two wenches making breadcrumbs. Their fire was so fierce as to fill the upstairs rooms with thoroughly real smoke. Three bedrooms are admirably fitted out, with special attention to fabrics and embroidery. In the Great Chamber was a complicated display of spinning, with much 'Come hither and witness'.

Nottinghamshire

Wollaton Hall

Eastwood:
D. H. Lawrence house

★ Birthplace of the writer, re-created as his childhood home

8a Victoria Street, Eastwood; museum, open all year

Do restored working-class cottages really tell us anything about those born there? Richard Hoggart, in his essay on D. H. Lawrence's birthplace, tries hard. He points out that Lawrence was an evoker of landscapes, notably those of Sicily, New Mexico and Australia. His home in this mining village, the setting of much of his early imagery, 'reminds us also that properly seen, inwardly seen; no landscape is in itself uninteresting, dull'. As Lawrence wrote in 'Piano', 'Softly, in the dusk, a woman is singing to me;/ Taking me back down the vista of the years.'

Eastwood certainly does Lawrence proud. The village's old library has various mementoes and the three houses where his parents lived have plaques. That in Victoria Street was his birthplace and home until he was just two. It is a tiny house on the side of a hill from which most of the original miners' cottages have vanished. The row is thus valuable if only as a relic of such houses. The adjacent corner house is a shop and visitor centre.

Number 8a is a small two-up, two-down. The Lawrences were poor but not destitute. Mrs Lawrence was an educated woman and a schoolteacher and kept souvenirs of her past. The front room of the house opens directly onto the street but is not mean. There is a lace tablecloth, china dogs, a few prints and 'Men of Harlech' on the piano. The front of the room has a large window, where Mrs Lawrence displayed linen and baby clothes for sale.

The kitchen is laid out for a meal, the range is lit and there is a sign that says simply 'Watch and Pray'. The carpet is a rag rug. On the stairs is the miner's helmet worn by Lawrence's father. The front bedroom has touches of gentility, a bowler hat, books, Bibles and rose-patterned wallpaper.

D. H. Lawrence
1885–1930

David Herbert Lawrence was born in Eastwood, the son of a miner and a former school teacher. He pursued a career in teaching until 1911, when the successful publication of his first novel, *The White Peacock*, allowed him to become a full-time writer.

During the Great War, Lawrence was suspected of colluding with the enemy because of his anti-war views and the fact that his wife was German. After the war, the couple emigrated and Lawrence spent his remaining years travelling the world. He died in Vence, France.

Holme Pierrepont *hall*

★★★ Ancient family home with Tudor and later wings

At Holme Pierrepont, 5 miles E of Nottingham; private house, open part year

Visiting Holme Pierrepont is not for the genealogically ignorant. Over the centuries, Pierreponts have been elevated, relegated and renamed. They have been earls, marquesses and dukes, Kingstons, Manvers, Newarks, Dorchesters and Brackenburys. Their names and titles are as confusing as the eras of architecture that jump out of the walls. At Holme Pierrepont, one can only relax and think of England, for this is a most English house.

What remains the home of a Pierrepont lies on the banks of the River Trent, approached down a track across a marshy meadow. The main entrance façade is that of a Tudor courtyard house. Once there were many courtyards, now just one.

The façade is of early brick, *c*1500, possibly from the King's Lynn area. It is a pleasant orange-red. The entrance range has two towers with ornamental battlements and strange alcoves on the outside. These could have been shelters for field workers since they back onto fireplaces inside. The range provided lodgings for visitors. The two ground floor rooms are divided by staircases, as in an Oxford college, and have generous fireplaces. Such early Tudor chambers still with their garderobes, doorcases, floors and fireplaces are rare.

'Holme Pierrepont ...
is a **most English house.**'

Left Restoration work in the 1970s repaired the decayed east wing and created a single Long Gallery overlooking the inner courtyard.
Right The oak staircase of c1660 was moved to its current position in the 1730s, following demolition of the state rooms in the west wing. Its woodwork has been painted white, concealing various repairs made in the 1970s.
Above Blind arches on the exterior of the house are positioned behind fireplaces on the interior, presumably to provide warmth to anyone seated in one of the external alcoves.

The upstairs room at the west end has close-studded partitions and is open to the roof. This has cusped wind-braces and is a fine work of late-medieval carpentry. Victorian costumes are on display. The dressing room has drapes by William Morris.

Beyond is the one remaining courtyard, only three sides of which survive. The original Great Hall would have been on the far side, and has been replaced by the present Victorian range. The court contains a knot garden, surrounded by a conservatory in the manner of a cloister. Its walls are a mix of plaster, exposed brick, clematis and rose, charmingly informal and picturesque.

The east range of the court is an architectural jumble. Surviving medieval and Tudor fragments emerge in the form of door lintels and fireplaces, notably in the splendid Long Gallery. Pierrepont portraits are everywhere, taking us back and forth over history. In the middle of the range is a sumptuous Restoration staircase with openwork balustrading, as at Thrumpton Hall (see page 123). (A Thrumpton owner is said to have let out a cry of joy on first seeing this stair, finding it inferior to his own.) Overlooking the staircase are two magnificent 1850s portraits of the 3rd Earl Manvers and his French wife. They once hung at Thoresby. Banished from the mammoth house which they created, they must hang in more modest splendour.

The reception rooms beyond have been restored by the present Pierrepont, Mrs Brackenbury, who has commissioned an admirable series of paintings depicting the house at various stages of its development.

Kelham hall

★ ★ Victorian neo-Gothic mansion by Gilbert Scott, with restored interiors

At Kelham, 2 miles NW of Newark-on-Trent; private house, grounds open all year

Kelham is a massive building on the outskirts of Newark, built mostly by Sir Gilbert Scott in his 'St Pancras' style. The house was begun by Scott in 1858 for the local MP, Sir John Manners-Sutton, but never finished. It became a religious retreat in 1903 and was extended in the 1920s with a new quadrangle and neo-Byzantine brick chapel. The older house contains the offices of the local council, but Scott's main rooms have been restored and, on wedding days, can even look magnificent.

The exterior displays Scott's love of Puginian Gothic. On reading Pugin, he said, 'Old things passed away and behold all things had become new; or rather modernism had passed away from me and every aspiration of my heart had become medieval.' This is what the anti-Goths most disliked about the Goths. Yet Kelham does not look medieval. Its harsh outline and even harsher materials came to epitomize municipal Victorianism, expensive but unforgiving.

The house is boldly asymmetrical, both in its plan and in its exterior details. The windows are extraordinary, with Scott trying out every conceivable variant of a Gothic opening. There are thirty-two different windows on the main façades. The interior, when it can be seen, is still in good shape. The original entrance is hidden behind a covered courtyard now used as a canteen. This has an Italian Gothic arcade round the sides, brick with banded arches and stiff-leaf pier capitals. The chapel is the council chamber. The drawing room is sumptuously neo-Gothic, with painted rib vaults rising from a central marble pier, gilded on a chocolate background. The ceiling has excellent floral stencilling.

All the main rooms are vaulted, as if Scott could not decide whether to build a house, church, museum or station foyer. Grandest is the music room, representing the Great Hall. It has a gigantic fireplace on one side, facing an arcade and gallery on the other. The vaulting is coloured and gilded, the capitals beautiful compositions from nature. This is Scott at his best.

Newark castle

⭐ Ruined remains of a Norman castle, overlooking the River Trent

Castle Gate, Newark-upon-Trent; museum, open all year

The revival of Newark's riverside has refocused the town from the market towards the site of the Bishop of Lincoln's 'fishing chalet' on the Trent. He was allowed to fortify it in the 12th century and build a tollbridge as source of revenue. The castle came to control this important river crossing, which was why it was destroyed late in the Civil War. The townspeople of Newark were allowed to use it as a quarry to repair their homes.

What remains prominent is the old gatehouse, among the largest in England from the Norman period. Although partly ruined, it towers over the approach to the town from the bridge, still with an undercroft and two intact floors. On the lower was a hall, later a chapel, with a study next to it. On the upper was probably the chaplain's chamber. The rooms still have Norman fenestration.

The courtyard beyond retains a magnificent curtain wall overlooking the river. This includes the outer wall of the castle's Great Hall. A pretty Gothic oriel survives, which must have given guests a splendid view over the valley beyond.

The remainder of the castle has been 'stabilized' as a municipal garden. It looked far more antique when covered with ivy, as shown in Victorian photographs.

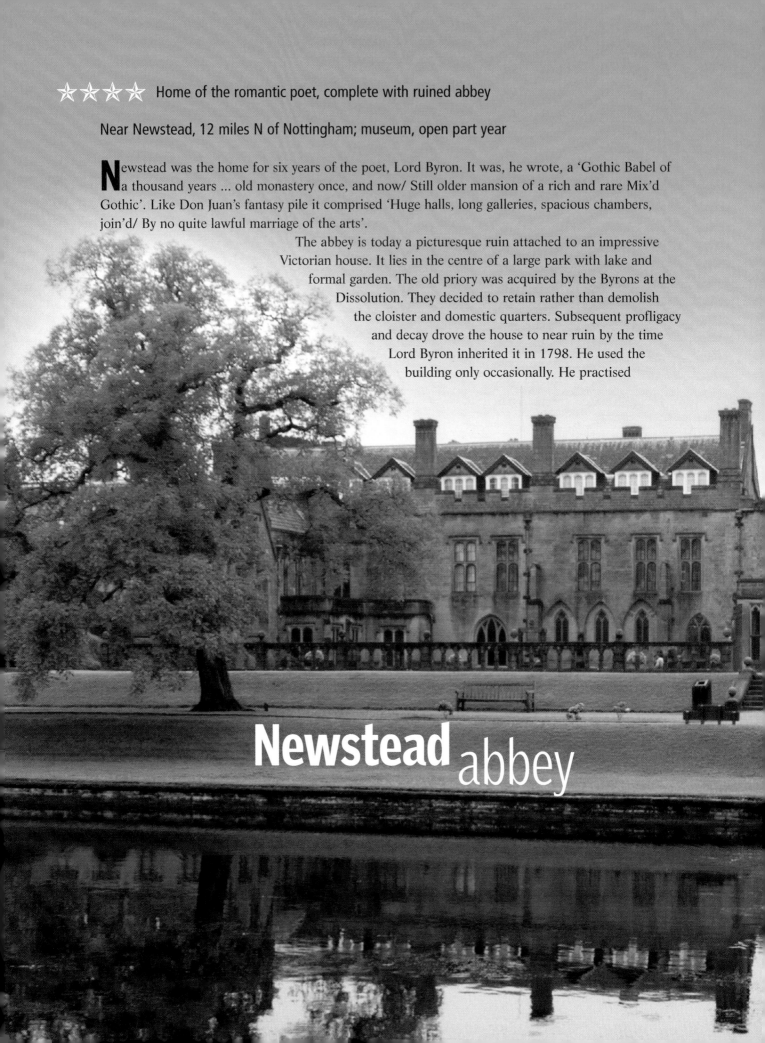

✩ ✩ ✩ ✩ Home of the romantic poet, complete with ruined abbey

Near Newstead, 12 miles N of Nottingham; museum, open part year

Newstead was the home for six years of the poet, Lord Byron. It was, he wrote, a 'Gothic Babel of a thousand years ... old monastery once, and now/ Still older mansion of a rich and rare Mix'd Gothic'. Like Don Juan's fantasy pile it comprised 'Huge halls, long galleries, spacious chambers, join'd/ By no quite lawful marriage of the arts'.

The abbey is today a picturesque ruin attached to an impressive Victorian house. It lies in the centre of a large park with lake and formal garden. The old priory was acquired by the Byrons at the Dissolution. They decided to retain rather than demolish the cloister and domestic quarters. Subsequent profligacy and decay drove the house to near ruin by the time Lord Byron inherited it in 1798. He used the building only occasionally. He practised

Newstead *abbey*

Right George Gordon Byron (1788–1824) became the 6th Lord Byron when he was just ten years old. He did not live at Newstead Abbey until 1808 and left it in 1814.

shooting in the Great Hall and had a bear and a wolf roaming free round the rooms. Servants had to be beautiful, all ugly ones being dismissed. When bankruptcy again threatened in 1817, Byron sold the house to his friend the Jamaican plantation owner, Thomas Wildman.

It is mostly Wildman's house we see today, as remodelled by the neo-Gothic architect John Shaw. Such was the expense of the conversion that, once again, ruination beckoned and Newstead was sold by Wildman's widow in 1861 to William Webb, a big game hunter and

friend of Dr Livingstone. By the time the house was given to Nottingham City in 1931, it had become a conventional Edwardian mansion.

It is now well maintained and the grounds are immaculate. The lake is as it was when earlier Byrons had their servants fight across it in miniature battleships, with live ammunition. The Byrons were plainly intolerable employers.

Shaw's main façade defers to the Gothic west front of the old priory church next door. The latter's blind arcading is balanced by the three tall bay windows of the Great Hall. Entry is into the undercroft, which rises to the Hall up a large neo-Gothic staircase. This Hall was once festooned with Webb's hunting trophies, its floor covered in lion and tiger skins. It retains a magnificent Victorian screen.

Beyond the Hall is Byron's dining room, oak-panelled and with a dazzling heraldic overmantel brought from a neighbouring Byron property, Colwick Hall outside Nottingham. It is like a hand of playing cards, heraldry surrounded with figures in frames. The furniture is Hepplewhite.

The West Gallery was installed by earlier Byrons over the monastic cloisters and looks

Right The carved neo-Gothic screen at one end of the Great Hall was designed by John Shaw for Thomas Wildman. William Webb, who bought Newstead from Wildman in 1861, left the Hall unchanged, although he had the walls hung with his big-game trophies, shot during his travels in Africa. Webb's daughter Augusta recalled a huge rhinoceros head hanging over the fireplace, bedecked with an 'incongruous wreath of holly' at Christmas time.

down on the peaceful cloister garth. It leads to the tower in which Byron himself slept. This has been re-created with Byron's own bed, decorated with reproductions of its drapes and coronets. The surrounding galleries and bedrooms were his friend Wildman's ideal of country house romanticism. They are named and 'themed' after English kings and queens, heavily panelled, with sumptuous overmantels and heraldic devices.

The climax is the Great Drawing Room, converted from the monastery's refectory, now called the music room. It has been restored according to its layout in 1840, with an original ceiling of 1631, and wallpaper by the heraldic designer, Thomas Willement. The room is dominated by a large portrait of an 18th-century Duke of Sussex. He has the face of a country solicitor and a costume out of Gilbert and Sullivan.

To the rear is a wing built in the 18th century on the site of the monastery reredorter or latrine. These smaller domestic rooms are decorated in 19th-century Gothic style. They include Byron's study with mementoes of his days at Cambridge. On the ground floor is a colourful chapel fashioned from the old chapter house.

From here on, medieval, Gothick and 19th-century Newstead merge into one continuous act of deference to the Middle Ages, as if to atone for its original monastic Dissolution.

Brewhouse yard

★ Row of houses with service quarters in caves cut from the cliff

Castle Boulevard, Nottingham; museum, open all year

Words fail me about Nottingham. In the years since the Second World War, this once-handsome hillside city has been variously punched, kicked and abused by its citizens. The new Nottingham is like a flayed skeleton to which patches of raw flesh cling bloodily in desperation.

One such is immediately below the castle rock, a row of 17th-century houses next to the Trip to Jerusalem inn. They belonged to the castle brewers, although they may have been built by clothiers using the river that once passed at the foot of the cliff.

The exterior of the row, dating from the 1680s, is of well-laid red bricks with projecting keystones. An arch is visible above the present entrance, presumably so a horse and cart could pass below. Like many of Nottingham's old buildings, the row has been seized by the council as a museum in penance for what is lost.

The museum vividly conveys the Nottingham that once occupied these houses. Living, sleeping and cooking areas are re-created, including an evocative bedroom. A series of workshops, such as for cobblers and barbers, are portrayed upstairs.

Typical of many early Nottingham houses are the service quarters at the back, cut out of the sandstone rock. Occupants during the war recall having to cover the cooking pots to keep out sand falling from the cave roof. A chimney rises from one of the caves to the castle above.

NOTTINGHAM

Wollaton hall

✯✯ Spectacular hill-top Elizabethan mansion by Robert Smythson

Wollaton Park, Nottingham; museum open all year

What to say of Wollaton? It was the architectural sensation of its age, a house designed by Robert Smythson, had who worked on so many great Elizabethan houses, including Longleat, in Wiltshire, and Hardwick Hall, in Derbyshire. Ostentatious in intent and cosmopolitan in decoration, Wollaton showed late Tudor England open to the Renaissance. Jan Siberechts' painting shows a glittering palace, with parterres and terraces, worthy of a Loire chateau.

Wollaton Hall was completed in 1588 for Sir Francis Willoughby, a fussy, learned and increasingly demented tycoon who had made a fortune from his estates and Nottinghamshire coal. What role Willoughby played in the house's design is not known. His ancestral home was at the foot of the hill and he clearly sought to overshadow it with a gigantic belvedere, rather as did Bess at Hardwick. According to his contemporary, William Camden, Wollaton stood 'bleakly but offering a goodlie prospect to beholders far and near'. Even today, surrounded by Nottingham suburbs, the house is startlingly bold.

The façade to the park is one of the most dramatic of any Elizabethan house in England. The central hall is embraced by suites of rooms and rises to a glass-sided gallery. Four towers guard each corner. What at Hardwick is a simple box of windows is here a restless and complex series of planes. The belvedere is like a look-out lantern above a galleon. Pilasters divide mullioned windows, dressed with cartouches of classical characters. The towers tumble with gables and strapwork, each a pavilion in its own right. The effect is both Renaissance and medieval.

Smythson is known to have drawn on Dutch and German pattern books, so much so that Sacheverell Sitwell found Wollaton 'like the worst excesses of the German Renaissance ... the strapwork ornament meaningless'. Smythson's biographer, Mark Girouard, sees Willoughby as a tragic and extravagant innovator, with an architect whose 'excitement went to his head'. The outcome was a sort of monster. Elizabethan guests driving across the park and rounding a corner of the terrace would have been 'amazed and excited but also appalled by the basilisk stare, the crash and glitter of that fantastic façade'. Yet the 16th century was the age of experiment. Nothing like Wollaton was to be attempted until Vanbrugh's essays in the Baroque more than a century later.

Wollaton suffered a fire in the early 17th century. The house passed to Lord Middleton who had the interior restored by Wyatville between 1801 and 1832 in his Windsor Castle style. Wyatville even

Below When Wollaton Hall was built it dominated the landscape around, looking down over Sir Francis Willoughby's original manor house and the local village. Today, the house is set in a 500-acre park, where herds of red and fallow deer roam, and the roof offers a prospect over the city of Nottingham.

'Even today ... the house is **startlingly bold.**'

Right Smythson's classical stone screen has survived in the Great Hall, adorned with Doric pilasters, strapwork and figures representing the exploits of explorer Sir Henry Willoughby, who died in 1554. The gallery above houses a 17th-century pipe organ, possibly made by Gerard Smith, and still blown by hand.

ripped out the panelling as a fire hazard in the event of an attack by a revolutionary mob, such being the temper of the times. His central hall survives with its fake hammerbeam roof and classical stone screen. Beyond are rooms that have been restored to the Wyatville period. The staircase also survives, with paintings said to be by Thornhill and Laguerre.

Wollaton was sold to Nottingham Council in 1924 and is now a natural history museum; stuffed animals and display cases jostle with ornaments. In 2007, a £9 million restoration programme was completed and the public can at last enjoy access to Smythson's belvedere, the Prospect Room, with its panoramic views of the park and beyond. The Regency Dining Room has been restored and re-created as it would have appeared during Lord Middleton's day and the Tudor kitchens have been refurbished as an 'interactive experience' with regular cookery demonstrations.

Ye Olde Salutation inn

✦ Medieval inn with restored Tudor exterior and ancient caves below

Maid Marion Way, Nottingham; public house

There is a certain rivalry between Nottingham's two oldest pubs, the Salutation and the Trip to Jerusalem, both dating from the late 12th century. Despite the latter's pilgrim origins, the Salutation is the older building. It sits alone on the hideously modern Maid Marion Way with a restored Tudor exterior and timbered walls. The name derives from the Angel Gabriel's greeting to Mary. The Puritans wiped the figures of both Gabriel and Mary from the inn sign, leaving two surreal hands shaking.

What is unusual about the inn is that beneath it lies some of the most evocative troglodyte dwellings in England. These are considered too delicate for pub use. Three levels of caves extend below the main bar, the lowest with a long open room with seating. The date of these caves is unknown, but they may go back to ancient Britons. They were later used for storage and brewing.

Off one of the passages is a surviving well and what is believed to have been a cockfighting pit, favoured sport of early gamblers. Nottingham is full of these ancient lodgings, none as yet reinstated to its possible ancient appearance.

NOTTINGHAM

Papplewick hall

★ ★ Late Georgian house with finely decorated interiors

At Papplewick, 7 miles N of Nottingham; private house, open by arrangement

The late Georgians liked their exteriors dull and their interiors exuberant. Papplewick dates from 1787. From the road, it is a severe box in grey stone with Ionic pilasters, handsome but restrained to a fault. The interior could hardly be more of a contrast, a decorative scheme by an unknown hand but clearly school of Adam. The owner was Frederick Montagu, a bachelor politician who inherited the property in 1770 and decided to build in the latest fashion. He also built a Gothick church as a landscape feature.

A descendant lost the house in a gambling debt in 1910. A decade later the suffragettes targeted Papplewick for arson in a bid for publicity, but succeeded only in scorching the floorboards. The house was later bought by the Godwin-Austen family and admirably restored. The best feature of the interior is the staircase fitted into an asymmetrical hall. One side is squared but the other rises in a fine curving sweep of stairs to a landing. With no children, Montagu commissioned only three bedrooms.

Papplewick's plasterwork is excellent, attributed to Adam's craftsman, Joseph Rose. It has been restored to what are said to be the original colours. The dining room ceiling has grapes and vine garlands in purple and green. The drawing room, in contrast, has had its plasterwork left not only unrestored but uncleaned. It looks more authentic but shows only that old plasterwork tends to get dirty. The walls are hung with local landscapes.

The last of the reception rooms is the library, painted turquoise with anthemions and classical medallions picked out in white. The bookcases are in exquisite Adam style.

Southwell Workhouse

Upton Road, Southwell; National Trust, open part year

Staff at the National Trust's 'not a stately home' project are emphatic that workhouses were not citadels of ghastly grim. They were, the Trust says, decent places to house the poor of the local community. As one inmate in the 1930s, May Croucher, recalls in the exhibition, her five years of childhood in the workhouse were a period of 'only happy memories'. This may explain why they have restored the interiors to look as if a modern architectural practice is about to move in.

Southwell Workhouse was regarded as the 'best preserved 19th-century workhouse in England' when it was bought by the National Trust in 1997. It had been built in 1824 by a local social reformer, the Reverend John Becher, to centralize the poor of forty-nine surrounding parishes, thus reducing the overall poor rate. It was widely influential.

Becher's concept was of humane accommodation but severe enough to be a stigma and deterrent to pauperism. It thus distinguished the Blameless and Deserving Poor, mostly the old and sick, from the Idle and Profligate Poor. Men, women and children slept apart. The work was menial, even humiliating. The old and infirm would be housed separately, as would overnight vagrants. Southwell would today be called a welfare 'one-stop shop'.

'Southwell would today be called a welfare 'one-stop shop'.'

Becher's building was impressive. It is in pink brick overlooking the fields outside the town, with the towers of Southwell Minster in the background. Behind is a courtyard with washrooms and workshops. The old latrines have been excavated. The laundry has been attractively refurbished with silhouettes of inmates on the walls.

The building interiors are little more than a backdrop for an audio-presentation. Only one room is restored with bed and clothing and another is left as it was in the 1970s, when used as an extension of the local old people's home. Most of the rooms are sparkling white and empty.

I cannot see the conservation ideology that forbids the refurnishing of these places yet fills them with modern equipment. Modern curatorship shouts louder at Southwell than do the Victorian poor.

Below The children's dormitory, like those for men and women, was housed in a separate wing. As in workhouses elsewhere, families were divided at Southwell. **Right** The inmates were further divided according to whether they were the 'deserving' or 'undeserving' poor. A system of 'double' staircases that interlocked but never met ensured that the different groups never came into contact with each other.

Thoresby hall

★★ Magnificent Jacobethan mansion designed by Anthony Salvin

Near Thoresby, 6 miles SE of Worksop; now a hotel

How are the mighty fallen. Thoresby was one of the great Dukeries estates. Here rose first a possible Talman mansion, then a Carr of York mansion. Then in 1864 the 3rd Earl Manvers and his French wife, Georgine, commissioned the elderly Anthony Salvin for an extravagant Jacobethan creation, fitted out in a riotously eclectic style. The eventual cost was £171,000, a stupefying sum for its day.

The house was occupied until the 1960s, then remained empty until 1980 when it was bought by the Coal Board for 'mining purposes'. These evaporated and Thoresby's fate became a cause célèbre. Eventually its contents were dispersed and the house sold for a time-share estate and Warner Holidays hotel. There are now fruit machines in the bar, photographic paintings on the walls and, on my last visit, transvestite entertainers promenading in the drawing room.

Thoresby was not an outstanding Victorian house. Compared with Salvin's Harlaxton of thirty years earlier (see page 50), Mark Girouard found it 'a depressing decline ... a cold house, dead in its handling and dead in its detail'. It was essentially a giant guesthouse, stripped of its original contents. The house is at least filled again with guests. The gardens bustle with people. On my last visit there was tennis on the tennis courts and cricket in progress beneath the south

terrace. The hotel additions are awful, sub-Marbella, but at least Thoresby is still with us, unlike its Dukeries neighbour, Clumber. Let us make the best of what we have.

The exterior is a Victorian evocation of Hatfield House in Hertfordshire. Turrets and pinnacles rise over canted bay windows. The iron gates to the entrance courtyard form a neo-Baroque screen. It is through these that one should enter, rather than along modern corridors from the hotel reception. Stone steps lead from below to the Great Hall.

This is still the most spectacular feature of the house. Although it has lost its armour, weapons and grand paintings, the Hall retains its hammerbeam roof and an immense chimneypiece surmounted by the Manvers arms. At the far end, a hidden staircase rises behind a stone screen to twin balconies, like opera boxes. The hotel has done its best to re-create a sense of Victorian clutter. There are antlers, candelabra, stained glass, tapestries and an old trumpet gramophone.

Of the stately enfilade of reception rooms facing the terrace only ghosts remain. French period ceilings survive in the Blue Drawing Room, complementing the Rococo wall-panels brought from Georgine's Château de Coigny in France.

In the old library is an overmantel by Gerrard Robinson, depicting Robin Hood and Little John beneath a giant tableau of the Major Oak in Sherwood Forest. For this alone, Thoresby is worth a visit.

Below The Great Hall at Thoresby is some 64 feet long and retains its air of Victorian splendour, with a minstrel's gallery and impressive hammerbeam roof. An enormous fireplace juts out into the room, topped with a carving of the Manvers coat of arms. The wood used in the Hall came from the surrounding estate, part of Sherwood Forest.

'Thrumpton sits in **eerie solitude** ...
It is a **precious survival.**'

Thrumpton hall

 Jacobean mansion with a magnificent Restoration staircase

At Thrumpton, 7 miles SW of Nottingham; private house, open by arrangement

The house is in an isolated enclave by the Trent, guarded by the cooling towers of the mighty Ratcliffe Power Station. A few hundred yards from the main road is an estate village, church, cricket field and moist riverside meadows. Thrumpton sits in eerie solitude under the lee of a protective escarpment. The house is still owned by Seymours, in line of succession from the Byrons of Newstead. It is a precious survival.

An old Tudor house was rebuilt by Gervase Pigot after 1607. His son enlarged and embellished it in the 1660s, with scalloped gables on the exterior and a new staircase and saloon inside. The latter, probably built to celebrate the Restoration, are exuberant works, more than a cut above the rest of the house.

The south entrance facing the hillside was reversed in the 19th century and the old forecourt laid out as an ornamental garden, now a blaze of roses. Access to the present entrance is through a dramatic series of brick arches. The outside of the house displays a feast of wavy gables, red brick and stone dressings.

'... the younger Pigot's **sumptuous** Restoration staircase ... is ... **a superb example** of its period.'

Far left The Restoration staircase was made of wood from the Thrumpton estate, using oak for the newel posts, elm for the balustrade and pine for the treads and risers. Incorporated into the carving are the arms of the Pigot family, as well as those of the Powdrells, earlier owners of Thrumpton.

Left The library is home to a collection of rare books. Thrumpton also has literary associations; the present owner is a novelist, biographer and descendant of the Byrons of Newstead. Mementoes of the Romantic poet, including his signet ring, are on display in the house.

The entrance is into the remains of the former Great Hall, which may once have spanned the entire cross wing of an H-plan. The old staircase by the kitchens would thus have risen from behind the screens passage. The house now is two rooms deep, with wings. The present hall is dark, as a hall should be, and the library behind, fashioned from the old entrance colonnade, is light as a library should be. It is a happy arrangement.

At the west end of the building rises the younger Pigot's sumptuous Restoration staircase. The proportions are of farthingale width, the balustrade of giant acanthus leaves embracing deer and heraldry. The staircase is of two storeys and a superb example of its period. The landing leads, somewhat unexpectedly, into the saloon. This is a serene and beautifully panelled room, classical in decoration and hung with family portraits, looking out over the garden.

Thrumpton has enjoyable roof leads. From here the crowded 17th-century gables, chimneys, dormers and gulleys merge into a magic forest with the hillside beyond. Attached to the house are 19th-century outbuildings admirably deferential to the style of the house.

Upton hall

★ Regency villa converted into a museum of clocks

At Upton, 5 miles W of Newark-upon-Trent; museum, open by arrangement

Upton Hall is a Regency villa of *c*1830 surrounded by cedars and lawns. It looks down at heel. The outbuildings are ramshackle and a greenhouse is home only to gargantuan weeds. Visitors take a perilous path to the back door and press an inconspicuous bell marked British Horological Institute. The door opens and reveals a wall of sound, that of a thousand clocks.

Upton is the only house in this book worth visiting for its noise alone. The exterior has a seemly portico. The interiors include a fine staircase hall, drawing room and ballroom. The hall rises the full height of the building into a dome and is magnificent, with a pedimented chimneypiece and acanthus frieze. All this is mere backdrop.

No inch of space is without a clock, every one wound up and in working order. The place is a pandemonium of ticking, whirring, bonging, burping and chiming. On the hour, all hell breaks loose. The clocks include grandfather, grandmother, pendulum, carriage, railway, alarm, wrist, quartz, talking, digital and doubtless others.

There is a Chinese dragon clock, a Congreve rolling ball clock, and a clock made entirely of wood. There is a counterfeit clock and a set of clock cigarette papers. On leaving, I heard the only sound I had missed within, that of a cuckoo.

Above A relief panel depicting simple countryside scenes, carved from wood, sits above the doorway in the dining room hall. Similar panels with different rustic views can be found above the doors of further reception rooms.

Winkburn hall

✦✦ Restored William-and-Mary mansion with Rococo carvings

At Winkburn, 6 miles NW of Newark-upon-Trent; private house, open by arrangement

'Left empty to decay at time of writing,' it says in Pevsner. Not any more. Winkburn is another modest English house taken in hand by a sainted descendant. It lies secluded from its village, the approach guarded by an old sycamore, stables and a small church. The view from the garden is so rural it might be a landscape by Stubbs. Inside are some of the most charming vernacular sculptures to survive from the 18th century.

The property had been granted by Henry VIII to his auditor, William Burnell, after the Dissolution and passed by descent to the Craven-Smith-Milnes family. The new house, attributed to William Smith of Warwick, was built around 1695, sold by the family in 1934 but reacquired as derelict in 1980. The 16th member of the family to live there has now restored it, with Mrs Craven-Smith-Milnes personally attending to the plasterwork.

The exterior is William-and-Mary, with generous sash windows and a much later top floor. The entrance is directly into the hall beneath the staircase, a sign that the original entrance was on the other side. The stairs are Restoration in style, with whorls of acanthus filling the panels, except that they are of iron, made in 1837. The ceiling carries a burst of Rococo plasterwork.

The main rooms have all had their plasterwork restored, the grandest being in the central dining room, previously the hall. The drawing room has an 18th-century stencilled ceiling. Many of the pictures have been generously lent from Welbeck as a boost to the restoration effort. Those in the stairwell are of the Stuart royal family, painted at the time of the house's rebuilding.

Winkburn's most remarkable possession is a charming set of carved relief panels, set above the doors in almost all the reception rooms. These are wood and of unknown origin, portraying domestic and architectural scenes. A man walks his horse home from work. Peasants besport themselves before Gothic ruins. In the library is a group of natives outside a wigwam near a grove of totem poles, a barque anchored in the bay. This may depict Captain Cook's voyages in the Pacific, widely publicized in the mid-1770s. Each panel is different. They are stylish, confident works, reminiscent of Lightfoot's work at Claydon House. They are a delight to find in so unobtrusive a house.

Worksop: Mr Straw's house

Edwardian suburban house, unchanged since the 1920s

7 Blyth Grove, Worksop; National Trust, open part year

This is a semi-detached tradesman's house in a Worksop suburb, of no distinction but absorbing interest. It is the sort of 'social museum' that will seem more plausible with the passage of time. The house was left to the National Trust by William Straw on his death, aged ninety-two, in 1990. It had been untouched since the 1920s, and remains today a 'time warp' of provincial England in the first quarter of the 20th century.

William Straw's parents were craftsmen turned shopkeepers. They ran a grocery business in Worksop High Street, prospering sufficiently to move from rooms over the shop into this house in Blyth Grove in 1923. It cost £767. The Straws' two surviving sons were well educated. One ran the business on their father's death in 1932 and the other, William, became a teacher. He did not marry, lived conservatively and put his savings into Marks & Spencer shares, leaving a small fortune of £150,000 on his death in 1990. He kept everything in the house as it was when his parents redecorated it in 1923. The National Trust have kept it that way.

Left The front door of No 7 Blyth Grove is the same as when the house was built in around 1905, with original stained glass.
Below The dining room at the front of the house faced south and was regularly used as a family sitting room. It was one of only two rooms in the house where a fire was regularly lit in winter; the Straw brothers economized on coal by placing bricks in the grate to reduce the size of the fire.
Right The parental bedroom of William and Florence Straw was left unchanged by their sons after Florence died in 1939; William had already died in 1932. The newspapers were laid over the bed to protect the covers from dust.
Below right An Axminster stair carpet was laid in the house in 1923, when the Straw family moved in, at a cost of £7 9s 6d. The design was inspired by Egyptian artefacts and influenced, no doubt, by the discovery of Tutankhamun's tomb the previous year. The original carpet has now been taken up to guard it against wear and replaced with a modern copy.

'... a time-warp of provincial England in the first quarter of the 20th century.'

The style is not, in truth, that of 1920s England but rather late Victorian. The wallpaper is mostly dark and the dominant colour of the interior is brown. In the front dining room, a local newspaper rests on the table. The light bulb that fell on William's plate during dinner was not replaced. It is still not replaced. The calendar stops at 1932, the year of Mr Straw senior's death.

The remaining rooms just 'remain'. Stacks of letters and old books fill the sitting room. Cupboards are filled with (non-perishable) food. Plates, sacks and boxes remain open. The store room is a complete mess. An Egyptian-patterned carpet leads upstairs to bedrooms more cream than brown. A bed is covered in newspapers to stop it getting dusty. Clothes remain beneath mattresses to stop them creasing. Pictures and even toothbrushes are in place. It is all odd and endearing.

Warwick

Charlecote Park

shire

Warwickshire

Arbury hall

★ ★ ★ ☆ Elizabethan house transformed by 18th-century Gothick style

3 miles SW of Nuneaton; private house, open part year

Arbury's interior decoration is England's outstanding evocation of 18th-century Gothick. George Eliot, whose father was agent to the Arbury estate, later described its decoration as 'petrified lacework'. She spoke of the house (Cheverel Manor in *Scenes of Clerical Life*) as 'growing from ugliness into beauty'. It surpassed even its progenitor, Horace Walpole's Strawberry Hill. The house was and is the seat of the Newdigates, Viscounts Daventry.

Sir Roger Newdigate was a Georgian antiquarian and scholar. Like Walpole, he assembled a group of enthusiasts to advise him on the new Gothick style and proceeded, over fifty years, to transform his Elizabethan house outside Nuneaton accordingly. He died at the age of eighty-seven with the house unfinished. His 'committee of taste' embraced the Midlands Gothicist Sanderson Miller, with Henry Keene, Henry Couchman and a changing group of craftsmen and stuccoists.

Above When Arbury Hall was transformed into a Gothick mansion in the second half of the 18th century, the Elizabethan Great Hall became the dining room. The portraits that line the walls reflect the earlier era, dating from the 16th and 17th centuries; chief among these is a portrait of Queen Elizabeth I by John Bettes.

Work on the interiors at Arbury began in 1750. Their essence is lightness, not the levity or frivolity often associated with the Gothick, but serious-minded lightness. Each of the principal reception rooms was redecorated in turn, mostly in variations on the Tudor fan vault. Since the Elizabethan structure remained, the vaults were entirely cosmetic.

Each room is a feast of decorative art. The brilliance of the stucco work is so delicate as never to be overpowering. It could not be further from the later Gothic revival of the Regency, of Nash, the Wyatts and Salvin, nor from the high seriousness of Pugin and the Victorian Goths. The style is well described by its historian, Terence Davis, as a branch of Rococo.

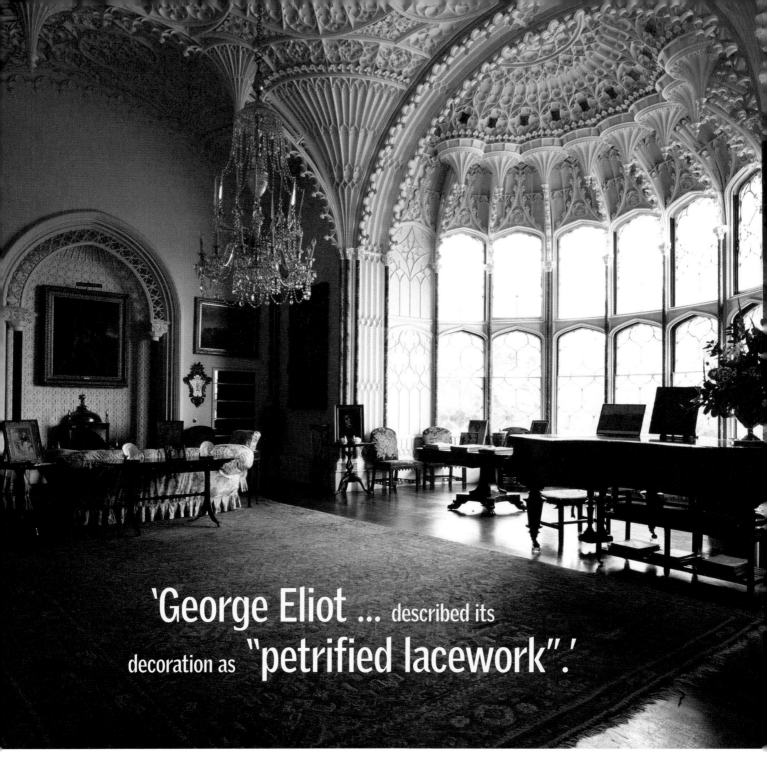

'George Eliot ... described its decoration as "petrified lacework".'

The exterior of Arbury is dull, an Elizabethan building uniformly medievalized. The entrance hall leads into a Gothic cloister built into the central courtyard of the old house, its atmosphere monastic. A modest but graceful staircase sweeps upwards in a vanishing curve.

The principal rooms begin with the chapel, not Gothic but 17th-century classical and thickly decorated with cherubs, swags and drops. That is the last we see of Rome at Arbury. From now on, it is the fan vault that wholly obsessed Newdigate. Four of these devices decorate the School Room, set round an ogival chimneypiece. The tempo quickens in the Little Sitting Room, with a panelled ceiling and receding window opening. This room is hung with 17th-century Newdigates.

With the saloon, the fan vaults mature, fluttering and dipping like the farthingales of ladies at a grand opera. The central panel is a burst of Gothick panelling, with a central pendant at the end of

which hangs a chandelier. The window opening is framed by a rim of delicious fretwork. These foaming waves of stucco are the masterpiece of Henry Couchman. Above the fireplace is a Reynolds of John the Baptist.

The drawing room is a wilder variant on the Gothick theme. The ceiling here is not fan-vaulted, except in the bow window, but barrel-vaulted. Yet the vault is entirely covered in Gothick panels that seem to ebb and flow as the eye travels their length. The extraordinary fireplace canopy, of ogival cinquefoils, is based on a tomb in Westminster Abbey.

The climax of Sir Roger Newdigate's handiwork is reached in the dining room. It is built inside the old Great Hall, the height allowing the fans to erupt from wall piers and spread over the ceiling in broad sweeps of plaster. Subsidiary fans decorate the small aisle. The walls are lined with canopied niches and statues. Two putti kiss over the fireplace. A magnificent portrait of Elizabeth I, appropriately holding a fan, adorns one wall.

The Elizabethan Long Gallery, with contemporary pictures and furniture, is something of a relief after this excitement; it is filled with Elizabethan furniture. The Dutch-gabled stables outside were reputedly designed by Christopher Wren, apparently for the price of a candlestick. Arbury is the more precious for being located in the dreariest of Nuneaton suburbs.

Baddesley Clinton

★★★ A medieval moated manor revived by its Victorian owners

At Baddesley Clinton, 8 miles NW of Warwick; National Trust, open part year

At the heart of Baddesley Clinton lies the beautiful image of Rebecca Dulcibella Orpen. Born in 1830 and living in County Cork with her aunt, Lady Chatterton, she captivated all and sundry. It is said that when the wealthy young Edward Dering came to ask permission to marry her from her fifty-three-year-old aunt, the partly-deaf spinster misunderstood. She told the world that Dering had asked for her own hand and she had accepted. Dering was too much a gentleman to withdraw. They both became romantic novelists.

Events now turned to Baddesley. In 1867, the pre-empted Rebecca married its owner Marmion Ferrers, the 'pleasantest and most genial old squire' in Warwickshire. When he caught an old lady stealing wood from his forest, he merely offered to carry it home for her. He would challenge poachers to boxing matches. Within two years of her marriage to Marmion, Rebecca had invited the Derings to share Baddesley with them. Soon Edward Dering was paying off mortgages and meeting expenses on the house.

The two couples, devoutly Catholic and immersed in the mid-Victorian artistic revival, became the Baddesley 'Quartet'. The house became a centre of literary and religious activity. It might have been a stage set for Gilbert and Sullivan's *Patience*. A painting of Dering has him looking like William Morris dressed as Oscar Wilde.

As a happy ending, when Lady Chatterton and Marmion Ferrers both died, Rebecca and Dering were at last married. She lived at Baddesley until her death in 1923, visitors noting a decrepit retainer still dressed in black with epaulettes. There were no children. Much of the furniture was sold to

Left The Great Hall was created by Henry Ferrers in the 1570s. The heraldic stone chimneypiece was also made on his orders but not moved to this position until the 1750s. **Below** The library dates from before Henry Ferrers' time. It is said that an indelible stain in front of the library fireplace marked the spot where Nicholas Brome murdered the local priest. Brome, who owned the house from 1483 to 1517, claimed he had killed the priest after finding him 'chockinge his wife under ye chinne'.

Above Henry Ferrers, the 'Antiquary', inherited Baddesley Clinton in 1564, when only fifteen years old. His bedroom dates from the early 17th century, when he returned from London and undertook most of the remodelling of the house. The fireplace was made around 1629; Ferrers's diary from that year records checking the joiners' work on 2nd March.

Baron Ash at Packwood House. Ferrers relatives struggled to keep the house going but eventually an endowment was found (ironically from the Baron Ash family) to give it to the National Trust in 1980.

The moated manor defies the enveloping villas of Birmingham's 'Marbella belt', in what claims to be a relic of the vanished Forest of Arden. Its charm lies first in its approach. An open drive through meadows reveals a simple 15th-century gatehouse, amended in the Jacobean period. It faces a bridge over a moat, a mix of stone, timber and romance. On the gatehouse wall hangs a monstrous processional sword. The inner courtyard has lost its old Great Hall, demolished to leave a gap with a view over the moat. The new hall is to the left. The half-timbered range directly ahead is a Victorian service wing.

The interiors must be seen as a manifestation of late-Victorian medieval revival, largely under Rebecca's influence. The new Great Hall is a lovely room, dominated by a stone overmantel encrusted with heraldic devices to the glory of the Ferrers. A fire burns in the grate. The pictures (most by Rebecca) depict the Quartet in various artistic poses. Rebecca's self-portrait hangs in the drawing room, painted in 1885, the year of her eventual marriage to Dering, but when still in mourning for Marmion. Both the dining and drawing rooms are warm and cosy. I am told that the sherry in the decanters is real but not for paying visitors (or Trust members) to drink. So for whom? For the staff?

Upstairs we pass through the rather denuded Ferrers and Blue Bedrooms with views out over the 'Forest of Arden'. Next door is the sacristy (with priest's hole) for the adjacent chapel. This is a panelled room converted from a former chamber in 1875. The reredos paintings are by various members of the Quartet and a fireplace stands ready to warm the worshippers.

The Great Parlour and the library were created by a 17th-century Ferrers known as 'the Antiquary' and his son. The parlour has a high Jacobean window beneath a barrel-vaulted ceiling. The furniture in the library is more Georgian, its books artfully scattered on the tables. The floor stain in front of the fire is said to date from the murder of a priest by a pre-Ferrers occupant, a badge of martyrdom on the old house.

Aston hall

★★★ Jacobean mansion saved by the city council

Trinity Road, Birmingham; museum, open part year

Aston Hall stands brave in a depressed quarter of Birmingham, its park and surrounding streets almost exclusively patronized by the city's Asian population. As a result, it can seem like a forgotten imperial palace in the suburbs of Lucknow or Calcutta. The great house in darkened brick and stone overlooks the old Birmingham–Lichfield road. Gloomy rooms and brooding corridors seem to gasp out their protest at the enveloping sprawl. There are plans for its dramatic renaissance, under way at the time of writing.

The Jacobean house was built by a grandee, Sir Thomas Holte, whose family had done well from the Dissolution of the Monasteries and who purchased himself a baronetcy from James I. He needed a house to match. Aston was one of the last so-called prodigy houses of the Jacobean age, designed to plans by John Thorpe and completed in the 1630s. The house was later rented by James Watt, son of the engineer, and after much argument acquired by Birmingham Corporation in 1864 as a museum, the first in what was to become a fine tradition of urban house rescue by civic authorities.

The view from the east is of a characteristic Jacobean façade, two storeys with an attic crowned with turrets, chimneys and gables. The other façades are more idiosyncratic. The south front has a long loggia, the west a splendid array of windows. Like Montacute, in Somerset, Aston was to be much imitated by Victorian revivalists.

The interiors are remarkable in quantity and quality. The Great Hall took its present symmetrical form late in the 17th century, when the screens passage was removed and its arches used for the doorways to the surrounding rooms. The fireplace with a scrollwork overmantel is where the screen once was. This reordering of the hall is flamboyant and must look wonderful when Aston is decked out for 'Jacobean evenings'.

The Great Parlour beyond is panelled from floor to ceiling and contains 17th-century furniture and a tapestry from Chastleton, in Oxfordshire. On the first floor is the formal suite of state rooms. These begin with the Great Dining Room directly above the Great Parlour, its frieze crowded with mythical incident. The furniture is Chippendale.

The lovely King Charles Room was used by the King for one night before the Battle of Edgehill, hospitality that was to cost Holte a three-day siege and a fine of £2,000. The Green Drawing Room beyond has fierce wallpaper, carefully copied from an 18th-century original, and another of the Jacobean fireplaces that are the pride of Aston.

The Long Gallery is the most magnificent room in the house. The strapwork ceiling is in place and the oak-timbered floor might be the deck of a galleon. The French tapestries are after that familiar 17th-century model, paintings by Raphael.

Aston continues with a wing used by the family in the 18th century, including the Chinese Room with japanned furniture and the Best Bedchamber now containing a state bed acquired by Aston in 1934. Former servants' quarters in the attic storey are open to the public, as is a charming small nursery with antique dolls. Back stairs lead down to the kitchen and servants' hall.

Below The Great Hall is not as Sir Thomas Holte built it in the 1630s. At some point towards the end of the 1600s the screens passage was taken out and parts were used to form the archways around the Hall. Aston suffered some damage during the Civil War when besieged by Parliamentarian troops; the Great Stairs still bear the scars of cannon shot.

Blakesley hall

✦✦ Restored Elizabethan manor house with sympathetic interiors

Blakesley Road, Yardley, Birmingham; museum, open part year

Richard Smalbroke dealt successfully in ironware, textiles and spices in the High Street at Digbeth, now a suburb of Birmingham. He inherited the Yardley estate from his father in 1575. The property passed out of his name shortly after his death but he is recalled in the city's ring road, the Smallbroke Queensway. He is also recalled in the house that he built at Yardley, Blakesley Hall.

Today the hall falls into the category of 'houses in most unexpected places'. We drive for ages through suburban Birmingham. Suddenly round a bend is a fine Elizabethan mansion in full black-and-white strip. The façade is a delight: a Great Hall with a gabled room over the porch and another over the dais alcove. To the left is a long, jettied and gabled Great Chamber wing. The half-timbering is close-studded below and diagonal on the first floor, a confident and jolly composition.

The inside has been well restored. The old table in the Great Hall, sold by the last private owner in 1932, was recovered through an advertisement in 1976. Good for Birmingham. The Great Parlour is dominated by a set of reproduction wall-hangings on canvas. Canvas hangings with dyed paintings on them were poor men's tapestries. As Falstaff patronizingly told Mistress Quickly, 'this waterwork is worth a thousand of these fly-bitten tapestries'. Very few survive, as they soon fell to pieces. These paintings, from the Bible story of Joseph and his Brothers, are by David Cuppnal and can be compared with rare originals at Owlpen, in Gloucestershire. They are a good example of bold reinstatement.

More hangings are in the Little Parlour behind, now a dining room, where loose blue and red drapes were used to conceal damp walls. At the top of the stairs is more decoration, here original, in the Painted Chamber. It has been meticulously uncovered on the plaster and timberwork but is, I fear, dull and archaeological compared to the new work. This was never great art and could surely be touched up to convey the original blazing colours. These are being reproduced in the wall-hangings of the bedroom at the rear, again a bold decorative project. The house is full of bulging walls, creaking floors, kitchens, dairy and pantry with hanging rabbits, all most atmospheric.

Selly manor

✦ ✦ Medieval house rebuilt in Cadbury's model village

Maple Road, Bournville, Birmingham; museum, open all year

Bournville was a planned garden suburb. Its creators were the Quaker Cadburys who had moved their old chocolate works from the centre of Birmingham to a hygienic and comfortable site in the countryside in 1879. The suburb, begun in 1893, was purely residential, a living community independent of the factory and not exclusively for Cadbury workers. The architect appointed in 1894 was Alexander Harvey, in close consultation with George Cadbury, who was also a keen gardener. Bournville preceded such better-known model settlements as Port Sunlight in Cheshire and Hampstead Garden Suburb in north London.

The dominant style was neo-Tudor, though neo-rustic might be a better term. In its midst was positioned a 'real' Tudor house, moved stick by stick from neighbouring Bournbrook. Cadbury re-erected it in 1912 as a central feature, surrounding it with a church, institute, meeting house and shops. With interest in medieval revivalism now booming, the Cadburys researched what had degenerated into a tumbledown row of workers' cottages, restoring the structure to full manorial glory.

The house is a fine example of a medieval hall house given a fireplace and bedrooms in the course of the 16th century. The original hall was in the centre of the building, its screens passage replaced by a chimneystack and its plaster walls replaced by brick. One wing formed the kitchen and the other, grander, wing the parlour and solar above. The latter was given its own outside staircase entrance, a rare feature. The interior is remarkable, not just for the purity of its restoration but for the furnishings. They include a Nonsuch chest (so-called because it is decorated with a painting of the now-lost palace), a mantrap and crossbows adapted for firing bolts or balls. The Tudor and Jacobean vernacular pieces, gathered by an active local trust, are one of the best collections of early furniture in the Midlands.

BIRMINGHAM

Soho house

⋆⋆ Late Georgian house of pioneering manufacturer

Soho Avenue, Handsworth, Birmingham; museum, open part year

Matthew Boulton was one of the true fathers of Birmingham's wealth. He was an 18th-century inventor and entrepreneur, still with the outlook of an enlightened Georgian improver rather than a Victorian capitalist. His Soho Manufactory was a workshop with many small processes and trade outlets under one roof. These were not located far from the proprietor's mansion so as to avoid pollution in the understandable 19th-century custom. They were next door across the lawn. Today, at half its original size, Soho House might be a comfortable vicarage, were it not for the numerous 'mod cons' designed by Boulton and his friends.

Soho House was built over two and a half centuries ago, and is now adjacent to a museum devoted to the birth of Birmingham industry. The surrounding community is more completely Asian and West Indian than any in Britain, and the building is in the shadow of a large Hindu temple. The museum is a good one and the house, though over-municipalized, has been well restored.

Boulton built the house in the 1760s and remodelled it with the help of Samuel and James Wyatt in the 1790s. The style is reminiscent of John Soane. The façade is a simple Georgian box, its entrance front decorated with four pilasters and a hipped roof. The walls are covered in rendered slate tiles. In the small garden is a thatched hermitage.

Below Born in 1728, Matthew Boulton set up his Soho Manufactory in 1760. In 1774, he went into business with fellow Lunar Society member James Watt as a manufacturer of steam engines.

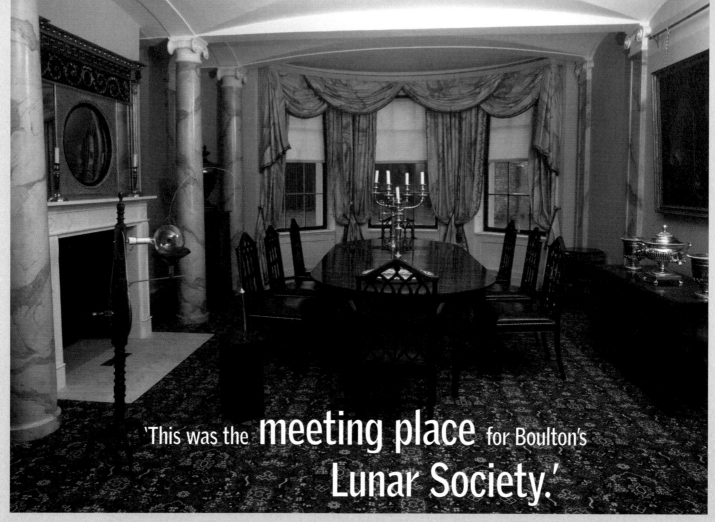

'This was the **meeting place** for Boulton's **Lunar Society.'**

Above The dining room at Soho House was established c1765, around the same time that Matthew Boulton completed his Soho Manufactory. He met regularly with like-minded local worthies who shared his interest in the new technologies of the day, such as the static-electricity machine standing by the fireplace.

The interior comprises a suite of rooms whose formal staircase was never completed. The diminutive entrance hall, with a screen of alabaster columns, is the one touch of grandness. There is a lobby with a 'Bramah' water closet. Like the steam-heated water supply and central heating released from holes in the stairs, these devices put Boulton's house in the van of convenience.

The hall leads into the dining room. This was the meeting place for Boulton's Lunar Society, a group of Midlands scientists and engineers who discussed inventions and new products and took forward the region's industrial revolution. The thin glazing bars on two of the windows are of 'eldorado' alloy, developed by one of the members, James Keir. The room has a gently groined ceiling and marbled pilasters. The calico curtains copy the pattern of this marbling. The Gothick dining chairs are by Gillow.

Downstairs are the breakfast room, drawing room and study, furnished with pieces by James Newton in the early 19th century. In the drawing room, Newton designed the base for one of Boulton's magnificent sidereal clocks. Here too are busts of Boulton by Flaxman and of James Watt by Chantrey. The study contains various inventions, such as a letter-copying machine and a barometer. Beyond is a fossilry, displaying various specimens of interest to the Lunar Society. This was truly an age when invention and development marched hand-in-hand with commerce and nodded occasionally in the direction of art. Upstairs are mostly bedrooms, well furnished but suffering from acute museumitis.

BIRMINGHAM

Charlecote park

★ ★ ☆ Elizabethan mansion with Victorianized interiors

Near Charlecote, 3 miles E of Stratford-upon-Avon; National Trust, open part year

Charlecote marks the point where southern England emphatically becomes Midlands. This is Henry James's 'midmost England, unmitigated England'. When he visited Charlecote, he viewed its 'venerable verdure' as being 'like backward years receding to the age of Elizabeth'. It was and is the house of the Lucys.

There have been Lucys at Charlecote since the 13th century. It was a Lucy who completed the new house in 1558, receiving Queen Elizabeth here in 1572. Young Shakespeare is said to have been caught poaching in the park, taking revenge on the relevant Lucy by making him Justice Shallow in the *Merry Wives of Windsor*. He complains to Falstaff that his friends 'have beaten my men, killed my deer and broke open my lodge'. The authenticity of this tale is debated in the guidebook.

Shakespeare's Charlecote is now no more than a ghost inside the house which was refitted and extended by George Hammond Lucy and his wife over the four decades following 1823. His decorator was the antiquarian glass-maker, Thomas Willement. Lucy spent £3,400 at the great sale

'Charlecote still shimmers from a distance ... like the backdrop to a Shakespearean history play.'

of William Beckford's Fonthill Abbey in 1823. His purchases included a pietra dura table in the hall and later the ebony state bed. At this time, Lucy also added a complete new west front beyond the hall, facing the River Avon. Willement produced ceilings and wallpapers, carpets, chair covers and bookcases. Charlecote is a supreme example of the Elizabethan revival.

From the mid-19th century, the house suffered a long decline. Lucy children were teased at Eton for their girlish surname and, when victims of the agricultural depression, sold paintings to pay bills. Heiresses forced reluctant husbands to call themselves Lucy to live there.

Finally the National Trust was summoned by the irascible Sir Henry Fairfax-Lucy, a man who left his children so hungry they had to escape to the local village to beg food. He knew he had come to an end, but his dealings over the house's transfer with James Lees-Milne were so appalling that when he died in 1944 in the course of them, 'nobody seemed to regret it very much'. His son had already been sent to Kenya as a punishment. This son now returned and tried to summon the servants by clapping. Soon there was none left.

At first, the National Trust doubted whether so completely victorianized a house merited its attention. But Charlecote is Charlecote. Across England, almost all Elizabethan houses are Victorian houses, and many Victorian houses are Elizabethan. The rest is archaeology. Charlecote still shimmers from a distance down its long avenue of limes, like the backdrop to a Shakespearean history play. In front is its jewel, the little Renaissance gatehouse doubling as a banqueting house and foil for the great façade beyond.

The interior is an excellent study in early-Victorian taste. The Great Hall is reached past the morning room, redecorated in dark brown, blue and gold. In the hall is the Fonthill table and an alabaster vase with carved doves from Italy. Family portraits crowd the walls. The dining room and library were built and furnished entirely in the reign of William IV, with Willement wallpaper and armorial glass. In the former room is that pride of every Victorian dining room, a massive sideboard carved in 1858 by Willcox of Warwick. It was, to Lees-Milne, a 'monster of inelegance, and ghastly curiosity of mid-Victorian joinery'.

Over the mantelpiece in the billiard room is a magnificent Batoni of the 18th-century George Lucy. The drawing room contains more pietra dura, ebony and a cabinet made for Beckford and acquired at the Fonthill sale. Upstairs are two guest bedrooms and a dressing room refurnished as in an inventory of 1891. The Ebony Bedroom, with its romantic view over the courtyard to the gatehouse, has a Beckford bed once slept in by Nelson and Lady Hamilton, albeit at Fonthill. It was made from a 17th-century East Indies settee.

The service wing and stables contains the scullery, kitchen, brewhouse, tackroom and travelling coach. These are displayed with typical National Trust meticulousness. In the park, Capability Brown has been allowed to survive, his landscape marrying house to river. The deer park still has the animals which Shakespeare may or may not have poached, and the Jacob sheep introduced by the Georgian Thomas Lucy in 1756. The present Sir Edmund Fairfax-Lucy, the artist, lives in a wing and has designed the new forecourt garden.

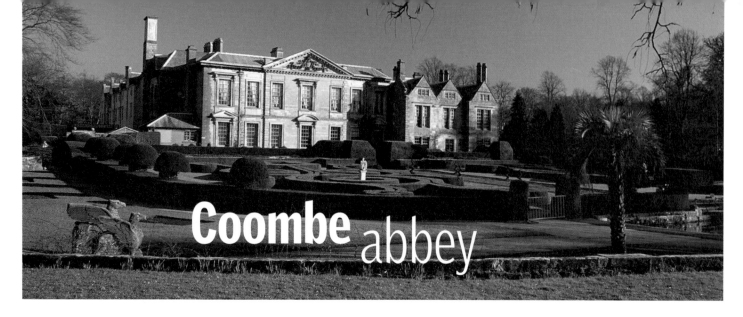

Coombe abbey

⍟ ⍟ Norman abbey and Restoration mansion with Victorian additions

At Binley, 3 miles E of Coventry; now a hotel

This is *Gormenghast* extravaganza. Arriving at what is now a hotel, visitors are greeted by plainsong chant and two giant pulpits, Bibles open at the ready. Icons and suits of armour jostle for space on the walls. Telephone boxes are converted from old confessional booths. Gift display cases are High Gothic caskets. Books are left lying everywhere. Somewhere an organ plays. Everything is dark, including the brows of the staff. An internal portcullis conceals the quay of an underground moat.

The old abbey was a Cistercian foundation which passed to Lord Harington at the Dissolution, then in 1622 to the Craven family. They retained it until 1923, when it was sold to a local builder and eventually to Coventry Council. It is now a 'No Ordinary Hotel', in the same group (and madcap style) as the Earl of Scarborough's Lumley Castle, in Durham.

The relics of the monastery are still visible in the cloister plan of the U-shaped forecourt and the red sandstone arches of the old chapter house. The cloister windows remain with, above them, Elizabethan windows and a variety of gables. All this was intended to turn an old monastery into a suitable residence for a Jacobean gentleman.

Onto this was later tacked a handsome range to the west, with large reception rooms and pedimented windows. This was designed in 1682 by the Restoration architect, William Winde, who probably also built Ashdown House in Oxfordshire for Lord Craven and the first Buckingham House (later Palace) in London.

The house survived in this form until 1862 when the then Earl of Craven commissioned W. E. Nesfield to adapt it as a large Victorian mansion and the family's principal seat. It became a rambling palace surrounded by a moat and ornamental gardens. Most of Nesfield's work was later demolished and the Wilde wing mutilated, to be supplemented in the 1990s by today's beefy, neo-Norman hotel extension.

The present interior, much of it original, is monstrously ill-used but can only be accepted on its own terms. The entrance, remarked *Country Life* recently, 'could easily lull the visitor into an expectation of quiet good taste'. Not the inside. Apart from the already described entrance lobby and hall, the main reception rooms are more respectful of their 17th-century antecedents, perhaps by virtue of heritage listing.

The north saloon has a huge Wrennish fireplace and plaster ceiling. The Walnut Room is rich in panelling. In a passage I tripped over a medieval bishop lying silent in prayer. Yet Coombe seems to us as Strawberry Hill or Cardiff Castle probably did to their contemporaries. Taste takes time to adjust – at Coombe, I imagine, quite a long time.

⭐ ✩ ✩ Tudor house, gently gothicized in the 18th century

Near Alcester, 8 miles NW of Stratford-upon-Avon; National Trust, open part year

Coughton is about Catholics. Of the Throckmortons of Coughton, it has been written that 'The family's strict adherence to the Catholic faith and their continued confrontation with authority seems to have condemned them to a less significant place in history than their abilities would otherwise have earned them.' Why some English families stayed Catholic and aloof from the mainstream of English Reformation, even to the point of treason, has puzzled historians. The medieval Throckmortons were wealthy Tudor courtiers, like thousands of others, but they opposed Henry VIII's divorces in the 1530s and since then have 'never capitulated'.

Throckmortons became a clan. They intermarried with other Catholics, maintained close links with the Continent and supplied monks and nuns to their Church. They were also implicated in various plots to usurp the English throne, from the Throckmorton Plot to the Gunpowder Plot. Treason, goes the saying, may be a matter of dates, but these Midlands rebels lived dangerously. As for Coughton (pronounced 'coaton') and the family's manor at Harvington Hall, in Worcestershire, recusancy proved a great conservationist. The chief change at Coughton, its Georgian gothicization, was probably carried out by the architect, John Carter, known as 'antiquity's most resolute friend'. The Gothic style was always associated, sometimes vaguely, with the Old Religion.

Coughton gatehouse is a typical Henrician tower. The former carriageway through its centre is now an entrance hall, fan-vaulted in the 1780s. This cold, stone chamber is relieved by such country house paraphernalia as antlers, an armorial screen, pewter and funny hats. Next door is a Georgian staircase lined with family portraits, many with grim faces seemingly set on martyrdom.

Coughton court

The domestic rooms are of a mix of periods and styles. The drawing room was allegedly the place where Lady Digby and her Jesuit friends sat eagerly awaiting news of the Gunpowder Plot. The turret windows next to the oriel carry the arms of the Catesby and Tresham families, both plotters. Over the fireplace is a portrait of the 18th-century Sir Robert Throckmorton, looking like a Bourbon courtier. It is by Nicolas de Largillière, who also painted the family nun.

The Little Drawing Room is beautifully adorned with sets of Worcester and Coalport china. Also displayed is a Mass cabinet, a travelling container for the Host. Its door reveals a stage set with mirrors, an exquisite work of kingwood veneer from the West Indies. From here, we climb to the tower room, dedicated to the Throckmortons' pedigree, and offering a view of the rear of the house, with its timbered Tudor wings extending into the fine garden.

The dining room, with 16th-century panelling, was formerly the Tudor Great Chamber. The room contains an old abbey dole gate and an armorial panel over the fireplace. Other curios include a chair made from 'the wood of the bed on which Richard III slept before Bosworth', and a cup from the wood of a tree 'under which Shakespeare once sat' in Stratford. The Tapestry Dressing Room is dominated by an entire wall depicting the Rape of the Sabine Women, an uncomfortable scene with which to fall asleep. More restful is the best set of gouaches by Ducros (1748–1810) to be seen in England: shipyard scenes and pavilions set deep in woods.

The house now becomes even more emphatically Catholic. The Tribune contains such relics as the supposed chemise in which Mary, Queen of Scots, was beheaded, and in which her dog was found

Above left A Flemish tapestry depicting the Rape of the Sabine Women covers one wall of the Tapestry Dressing Room. **Above** The Tapestry Bedroom became the home of Elizabeth Throckmorton, the last Abbess of Denny Convent, who returned to Coughton in 1539 on the Dissolution of the Monasteries. She lived there with two of her nuns until her death in 1547. **Right** A framed record of the wager between Sir John Throckmorton and John Coxeter of Newbury, commemorating the making of a coat that began the day as wool on the backs of two sheep at sunrise and was completed by sunset on the same day – 25 June, 1811.

whimpering hours after her death. Here is Catherine of Aragon's cope and an alabaster relief of the Nativity. Beyond is the saloon, formed in 1910 from the 17th-century chapel and reached down the fine carved staircase brought from Harvington Hall. Here we can see the coat made in 1811 for a wager that it was impossible to make Sir John Throckmorton a coat from two live sheep between sunrise and sunset. The wool was cut, spun, spooled, warped, loomed, woven, burred, milled, rowed, dyed, dried, sheered, pressed and tailored in 13 hours 20 minutes – and the wager won.

The new garden at Coughton 'sympathetically echoes the Tudor architecture of the house'. The River Arrow has been diverted into pools and lakes, watering a delightful bog garden.

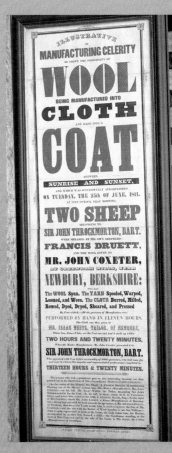

Ettington park

This Victorian Gothic confection is located on a platform overlooking the River Stour. It has suffered for much of its life for being 'over-the-top'. Like many such houses, it had a tragic 20th century, being hospital, school, hotel and disco, until wrecked by fire in 1980. It has since been well restored as a hotel, glorying in the dubious accolade of being England's 'most haunted'.

The house belonged to the eccentric Victorian Evelyn Philip Shirley, descendant of the 1st Earl Ferrers. It was on the site of a village that the family had owned since before the Norman Conquest, but had since removed. The family were devout Catholics. The 4th Earl Ferrers was the last aristocrat to be hanged, at Tyburn in 1760, for murdering a rent collector. He claimed a peer's silk rope.

Evelyn Shirley was the local MP, but he immersed himself in genealogy, archaeology and architecture, appearing as Ardenne in Disraeli's *Lothair*, 'a man of ancient pedigree himself, who knew everyone else's'. In 1858 Shirley commissioned the architect T. F. Pritchard to redesign his house in Ruskinian Early Gothic. The walls were embellished throughout with friezes of his family's history. The exterior is a mass of mid-Victorian stone polychromy, known as 'streaky bacon style' but here well controlled and delicate. It honours Ruskin's belief in sculptural detail, to 'point a moral or adorn a tale'. Ettington is Victorian architecture at its most ideological. The combination of polychrome brick and extensive sculptural decoration is matched only by Teulon's Elvetham Hall.

The entrance has a *porte-cochère* fronting a Gothic screen. Behind rise three gables flanked by one square and one rounded tower, with wings thrusting forward on either side. The windows are pointed or flat-headed. The right-hand tower turns the corner to the garden front where it confronts an even more splendid tower festooned with monarchs and gargoyles.

Here everything is balanced yet never symmetrical, each Gothic feature striving to outdo its neighbour. Panels depict Shirleys in numerous gallant and pious exploits, including killing Saracens in the Holy Land.

The interior is more heavy-handed. The modest entrance hall is blessed with a large Elizabethan fireplace with logs blazing beneath the arms of the Shirleys. The library contains Gothic bookcases and a Decorated Gothic fireplace.

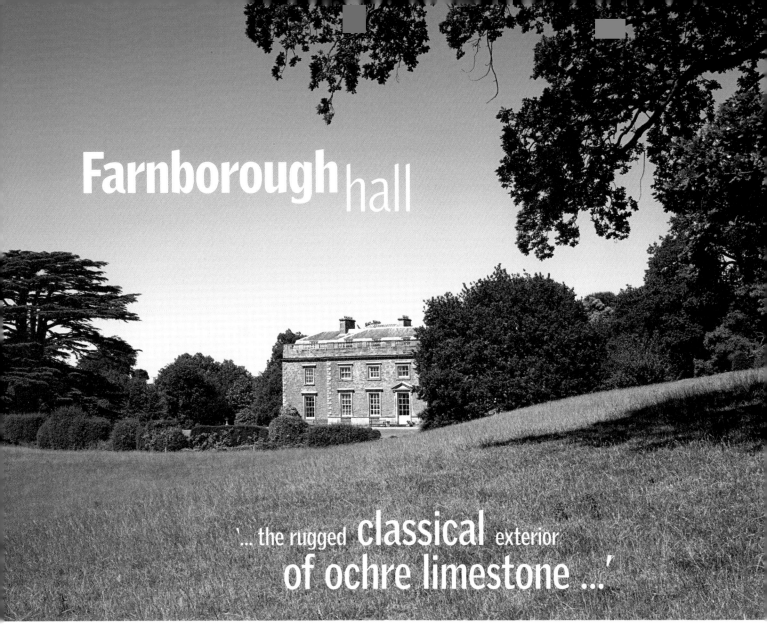

Farnborough hall

'... the rugged **classical** exterior of ochre limestone ...'

✫✫ A William-and-Mary house refashioned in the early 18th century

At Farnborough, 6 miles N of Banbury; National Trust, open part year

William Holbech went on the Grand Tour in the 1720s and returned with Canalettos, Panninis and a large collection of Roman busts. He promptly refashioned along classical lines the house his family built in the 1690s. He also refashioned its park to replicate a landscape in the Roman *campagna*.

The house sits secluded in a dell, russet-walled, with bold classical windows and parapet. A handsome terrace walk stretches nearly a mile to the distant hills, Warwickshire as a plausible version of Italy, at least in a dry summer. The scene is dotted with temples, a pavilion and an obelisk. Although owned by the National Trust, the house is still occupied by the Holbech family.

The redesigned house was almost certainly by William Jones, surveyor to the East India Company (see Honington Hall, page 157), although the family vigorously maintain that Sanderson Miller was the architect. The rooms were decorated with Rococo plasterwork by William Perritt in the 1740s. The stucco is as rich as that at Ragley and some may be attributed to the great Italian stuccoist, Francesco Vassalli. The contrast at Farnborough is startling between the rugged classical exterior of ochre ironstone and the warm, delicate interior.

The entrance hall, staircase and two rooms are open to the public. The hall is chiefly remarkable for the brackets and niches designed to carry the Roman busts. These are of emperors and noble ladies, forming one of the largest such collections remaining in their designed setting. The ceiling has panels with Rococo designs.

The Georgian dining room beyond was built into what had been originally the rear courtyard of the earlier house. The plasterwork is outstanding, not only on the ceiling but also round the panels framing Holbech's copied Canalettos and Panninis (unfortunately the originals were sold in 1929). The dining table is surrounded by 'splat-backed' chairs, intended for removing boots. They are remarkably comfortable.

The staircase hall has more Rococo plasterwork and busts in niches. Here the ceiling oval is earlier, dating from the William-and-Mary period, with garlands of fruit and foliage, almost vulgar against the adjacent Rococo. The stair treads are shallow, as was the custom *c*1700. There is also fine plasterwork in the Oval Pavilion, reached by a long trek up the Terrace Walk.

Below The entrance hall at Farnborough is overlooked by a series of Roman busts, set on plinths in oval niches. The statuary was part of a collection of sculpture brought back by William Holbech after his Grand Tour of Italy; he returned with some 29 marble busts and eight marble bas-relief panels which he incorporated into the decor of his home.

Honington hall

✦✦✦ Red-brick Restoration mansion with important Georgian interiors

At Honington, 10 miles S of Stratford-upon-Avon; private house, open by arrangement

'I have lost my balls again', was the regular cry of one of the 20th-century owners of Honington, Sir Charles Wiggin, to the local police as vandals tipped his bridge ornaments once again into the River Stour. It enlivened an otherwise dull beat. The old man was struggling to maintain this jewel of a house and vandals were the last thing he needed. His balls are still with us and his family live in the house to this day.

Honington lies in a lost landscape where the Cotswolds peter out yet the Midlands has yet to begin. Here England momentarily loses a sense of direction. The park has a charming gatehouse in the village in the style of Wren. The house itself sits at the end of a graceful drive, redbrick with white eaves and a hipped roof. It is a picture of quiet dignity.

The house was built by a London lawyer, Henry Parker, who married into the Hyde family and became MP for Evesham. The date is *c*1682 and the architect unknown. The house was sold in 1737 to Joseph Townsend who, in the 1740s and 50s, embellished it with curved screens and reordered and decorated the interior. He arranged Roman emperors on the façades, like the busts at Farnborough (see page 155). The architect, who also worked at Farnborough, was probably William Jones.

The 1750s were a period of innovation in English interiors, notably in the Midlands. The hall at Honington is sensational. Townsend created a screen between it and a new stairwell beyond, forming a sort of *porte-cochère* to the octagonal saloon beyond. The ingenuity is reminiscent of Mawley Hall, in Shropshire, or John Chute's work at The Vyne, in Hampshire; an amateur conversant with architectural language and able to instruct his craftsmen with assurance. The craftsman was probably Charles Stanley, although William Perritt and Thomas Roberts of Oxford are also mentioned.

The hall is yellow but almost every inch is coated in foaming white Rococo. Over the fireplace an ornamented panel contains not a painting but a bas relief. The ceiling roundel is a giant starburst. The stairwell drips with plaster foliage as if still wet from the rain.

To the left of the hall is the Oak Room, now the Wiggin family sitting room. The original 17th-century panelling has been retained but with a Georgian doorcase of sumptuous grandeur. Two reclining cherubs rest on its pediment while winged sphinxes (possibly later additions) sit over its lintel. This door is fit for an emperor.

The pink-walled boudoir leads into the octagonal saloon, executed in 1751. It is hard to overstate the beauty of the Honington Octagon. Classical doorways crowned with cherubs are set against blue wall panels. These are interspersed with swirling Rococo pier-glasses and plaster swags and festoons, depicting the seasons, Aesop's fables, the elements and cornucopia.

'It is hard to overstate the beauty of the Honington Octagon.'

Above, a coffered semi-dome rises to a painting of Acis and Galatea by Luca Giordano. Each of the rosettes in the coffers is a different design. Three of the eight walls are windows, giving views over the valley outside. Sacheverell Sitwell, encountering this room for the first time, rated it with the great palaces at Holkham and Houghton, both in Norfolk.

The design of the Octagon and other alterations are attributed to an amateur architect, John Freeman of Henley, whose estimate stipulated £100 'for a little carving, gilding and embellishment for the ladies'.

Left The entrance hall at Honington is lavishly decorated with Rococo-style plasterwork. A stucco panel depicting a suitably classical scene forms the overmantel; cupids occupy the space above the doorways. **Below** The Octagon was the work of John Freeman, an amateur architect who seems to have designed chiefly garden buildings, and it is the only example of his architecture to have survived outside his estate at Fawley Court in Buckinghamshire. The room replaced an earlier saloon and loggia and measures some 30 feet in diameter.

Kenilworth castle

★★ Ruins of a medieval fortress where the Earl of Leicester entertained Elizabeth I

At Kenilworth, 4 miles N of Warwick; English Heritage, open all year

There are those who regard Kenilworth as the definitive English castle. It shares with Rochester, in Kent, the distinction of having suffered a real medieval siege in the 13th century. But its glory lies in its occupancy by Robert Dudley, Earl of Leicester, and his nineteen-day entertainment of his adored Elizabeth I in 1575. The event was immortalized by Walter Scott in *Kenilworth* and made this a place of huge Victorian appeal. The castle has never lacked for romance, except perhaps now.

The Norman keep was held in 1266 by rebel supporters of Simon de Montfort against Henry III. The resulting assault lasted nine months. Siege engines came from Nottingham, boats to cross the moat were summoned from Cheshire and arrows from the Forest of Dean. Every stratagem of war was employed, from excommunication to the plague. At Kenilworth's eventual surrender, the defenders were allowed to walk free.

The castle was later turned into a palace by John of Gaunt and embellished by Dudley to receive the Queen. The castle never recovered from his downfall and was slighted in the Civil War. In 1937 it was bought as a ruin by John Siddeley, Lord Kenilworth, and is now cared for by English Heritage. The great defensive mere, or lake, has been drained and the ruins tamed with lawns.

The approach is over what would have been the causeway. The outer walls are intact and the keep of the old castle retains its original proportions. Round it are the ruins of Gaunt's palace, including the vast Great Hall with Gothic doorway and bay window. To the left of the inner enclosure is the three-storey block built by Leicester for Elizabeth. The windows are large, the rooms spacious.

In the outer court opposite is Leicester's new gatehouse, still intact but closed to visitors. Its entry is a pretty classical portal decorated with Tudor roses and containing a curiously ribbed arch. It contributes a dash of Renaissance charm in this awesome medieval place.

Middleton hall

⭐ A collection of historic buildings round a courtyard

At Middleton, 4 miles SE of Tamworth; private house, open part year

The country between Birmingham and Tamworth is much abused. Poor Middleton Hall is a victim of this, despite efforts being made to rescue it. The house was home in the 17th century to the naturalist Francis Willoughby, a founder of the Royal Society. More remarkable today is the group of buildings round a courtyard to the rear, dating from the 13th to the 17th centuries.

The house itself has a plain 18th-century façade to the garden. Behind is the former Great Hall, dating from 1530, georgianized and with a theatrical staircase rising to a balcony between incongruous fluted columns. Poor copies of ancestral pictures gaze down from the walls. Embroidery panels upstairs depict the history of Sutton Coldfield.

The buildings round the courtyard behind are being restored. The south wing is a 17th-century domestic hall with solar, while the eastern range is made up of the 13th-century stone manor house, a 17th-century lodging house and a 16th-century jettied building with a close-studded timber frame. There was another Tudor building between the jettied house and the Great Hall, but his was demolished in the 1920s. They should form an exciting group when fully reinstated.

Packwood house

⭐⭐⭐ Tudor manor house revived in the 20th century

9 miles NW of Warwick; National Trust, open part year

The yew garden at Packwood is a horticultural Karnak. The columns of the Egyptian temple of Amun are said to come alive at dusk with the spirits that inhabit them. The same goes for these mighty yews. They are called the Sermon on the Mount, listeners attending the distant preacher, nodding, muttering and growing increasingly excited in the wind. Packwood in the Civil War harboured both Cavaliers and Roundheads. These can only have been Roundheads.

The house is now a monument to the 20th-century manorial revival. It had belonged to the Fetherston family from the 15th to the 19th centuries. Charles Fetherston, inheriting in 1815, insisted that everything he ate, drank, used and wore be grown on his land and made within his walls, even his shoes. This early sustainability did not last. The house fell to ruin and was eventually bought by a Midlands industrialist, Alfred Ash, in 1905. His son, Baron Ash, made its restoration his life's work. Everything we see of the interior was inserted in the 1920s and 1930s, garnered from decaying houses across Britain. The connoisseurship was immaculate.

Baron Ash (a name not a title) was of a generation which disliked Georgian and abominated Victorian. His antiquarianism was aesthetic. There is nothing proletarian about Packwood's Tudor, and none of the political correctness of Ruskin or Morris. Ash was obsessively neat. He hated a book incorrectly set on a table. His clothes were always pressed, proving to James Lees-Milne 'that he was not really a countryman'. A guest arriving a minute late for an appointment or even a meal was sent away. As for the galvanized iron foundries that were the source of his family's wealth, they were never, ever to be mentioned under his roof.

So what are we to make of Ash's creation, a home or a museum? It was undoubtedly his home, but that of a man so fastidious that only a museum would do for a home. Since National Trust conservationists are Baron Ash reincarnated, perhaps we cannot complain. None of them can tolerate a cobweb. Yet Ash's motto was the admirable, 'Not for us but for everyone'.

The public road to Packwood turns through gateposts and appears to be a private drive. To the left are the billowing rollers of the yew garden. Beyond is the rich façade of the house, a series of Elizabethan gables and chimneys, much restored.

Below Baron Ash and his architect Edwin Reynolds created the Long Gallery in 1931–2 to link the original Great Hall to the new one. The floorboards were rescued from Lymore Park in Wales, the panelling and overmantel from Shaftsmoor in Birmingham, two houses that were in the process of being demolished. The fireplace was from a house in Chipping Norton.

Above The drawing room is part of Jacobean Packwood, with the original panelling and ceiling beams still in place. In front of the fire stands an 18th-century walnut wing armchair, covered in yellow silk, and on the table next to it is a Rockingham cup and saucer; the chair and china were both used by Queen Mary during her visit in 1927.

Two words sum up the interior, wood and tapestry. Wood came from the adjacent Forest of Arden. Tapestries came from anywhere Ash could find them, notably superb Brussels works acquired from neighbouring Baddesley Clinton. Entrance is to the screens passage, leading to the hall which has a floor laid in chevron pattern. This was acquired from another house, Lymore Park in Montgomeryshire, where it had subsided into the basement during a dance. The Powis family subsequently threw it out in embarrassment.

From the hall Ash led a gallery to an outlying barn, which he reconstituted as a second, more formal Great Hall. He acquired an enormous table from Baddesley, more tapestries and a fireplace from Stratford 'in front of which Shakespeare may have sat'. Hatchments and banners from his proud term of office as High Sheriff of Warwickshire adorn the roof. A stone staircase leads to the bedrooms, beautifully furnished and named after distinguished visitors.

Queen Mary's Room, with a child's setting of table and chairs, was 'at her disposal' during a brief visit in 1927. Queen Margaret's Room is named after a bed in which she may have slept (somewhere else). Ireton's Room, with its solid Parliamentary four-poster, was allegedly occupied by the colonel before the Battle of Edgehill in 1642.

The downstairs drawing room, study and dining room are those of the original house, albeit swamped by imports. The pictures are not distinguished, being chosen rather to fit in than impress, an admirable aim. The dining room has flame-stitch hangings and Flemish window roundels.

The garden at Packwood was described by Geoffrey Jellicoe as having 'worldliness combined with a curious vague, indefinable mysticism'. The layout is Jacobean, an orderly sequence of Fountain Court, sunken garden and wilderness beyond, all overlooked by gazebos. Beyond is the ever-stern Sermon on the Mount. The yews rise up the hillside towards the mysterious mound where stands a single mighty yew, the master, preacher and monitor of the foibles below.

Below The bed in Queen Margaret's room came from Owlpen Manor, in Gloucestershire, and was bought by Baron Ash in 1927. It is claimed that Margaret of Anjou, wife of Henry VI, slept in the bed before leading the Lancastrian army at the Battle of Tewkesbury on 4th May, 1471. The canopy and hangings are of a much later date.

'... a monument to the 20th-century manorial revival.'

Ragley hall

★★★☆ Mansion by Hooke, completed by Gibbs, and heroically restored

8 miles W of Stratford-upon-Avon; private house, open part year

Ragley is the home of the Marquess of Hertford and he does not mind who knows it. Like Beaulieu, in Hampshire, and Woburn, in Bedfordshire, this is a country house which sells itself on dynasty, here that of the Seymours. Big houses in modern England have learnt to survive either on bureaucracy or on egotism. I prefer egotism. The modern family mural that adorns the south staircase hall is an astonishing assertion of 20th-century heredity.

This is the more remarkable since, in 1930, there were plans to reduce Ragley to a villa and in 1951 the family's trustees proposed to demolish it

Left Ragley Hall was begun by Viscount Conway in 1679, the same year that he became Earl. In 1750, when a later Lord Conway became Earl of Hertford, the architect James Gibbs was called in to complete the house. Although the Great Hall was built by Robert Hooke, the decoration was designed by Gibbs.

altogether. The determination of the then twenty-one-year-old 8th Marquess to save it was assisted by quantities of public money. 'A house is a life sentence,' he said in a phrase echoed by many a house owner. He served it until he died in 1997, a sentence to be continued by his son.

Ragley has a conventional exterior but sensational interior. It was first designed by Wren's associate, Robert Hooke, in 1680 but not completed until the mid-18th century under James Gibbs and James Wyatt. To Gibbs, we owe the Great Hall, and to his Italian craftsmen, especially the Artari brothers, the astonishing plasterwork in the main reception rooms. Wyatt later added the central portico and flowing front stairs, a touch of late-Georgian Baroque.

Entry into the house is under the portico, directly into the two-storey Great Hall. The impact is immediate. Ragley's pink and white hall is the nearest an English grand chamber came to architectural, rather than decorative, Rococo. Fluted pilasters rise to an upper storey of blind arcading, swags, busts and urns. The ceiling medallion is of Britannia holding a spear. French windows allow light to stream in from the portico and the whole is boldly coloured pink. The plasterwork was not begun until 1756, so Gibbs would never have seen his design realized.

The main reception rooms are each an essay in paint and plaster. The music room is in varieties of blue, again with Gibbs plasterwork. The breakfast room is in orange with a Rococo overmantel. The dining room goes for a vivid yellow. Everywhere the colours are made to talk. The wall panels are designed to frame portraits by Hoppner and others. Only in the north staircase hall does boldness get the better of common sense. A shocking gash of blue and yellow by the modern artist, Ceri Richards, diminishes the wallpaper round it and jars with the architecture.

The decorative features introduced by Wyatt in the 1780s are less extrovert, closer to the delicacy associated with Wyatt's rival, Robert Adam. The crimson damask of the Red Saloon, with a beautiful painted ceiling, is based on the original colour. The Green Drawing Room is hung with Seymour portraits by Reynolds, and two exquisite Chinese Chippendale mirrors.

Left Portraits in the Green Drawing Room chart the history of the Seymour family. Descended from Edward Seymour, 1st Duke of Somerset (and brother of Henry VIII's third wife, Jane Seymour), the family claim the Norman Guy de St Maur as an ancestor. **Above** The walls of the staircase hall record more recent family history. They were painted between 1969 and 1983 by Graham Rust and include portraits of the 20th-century Seymours and their friends.

The great south staircase hall, filled with the famed *trompe-l'œil* mural by Graham Rust, was executed between 1969 and 1983. It depicts the then Hertford family in modern dress but in a scene after the manner of Thornhill. Although controversial, the Baroque design fits into its Georgian setting, responding to the off-white shades of the doors and balusters. Not everything works, notably the kitsch ceiling roundel of *The Temptation*, but the composition is complete and executed with panache.

The Victorian Hertfords neglected Ragley and spent their money accumulating one of England's greatest art collections. This was passed not to the house but to Richard Wallace, illegitimate son of the 4th Marquess, who lived in Paris. Wallace left it, with his London house in Manchester Square, as the Wallace Collection. As a result, Ragley's pictures are disappointingly poor. With hundreds of paintings in store, I cannot believe the Wallace could not loan some works.

Stoneleigh hall

✦ ✦ ✧ Restored masterpiece by Smith of Warwick in a Repton landscape

Near Stoneleigh, 4 miles S of Coventry; private house, open part year

Stoneleigh is a triumph of 18th-century building and landscaping, and of valiant 20th-century rescue. The seat of the Leigh family since 1561 seemed doomed after a fire in 1960. It might have become a golf club, offices or a ruin. Now controversially restored, it is regaining some of its former splendour. The family set up a preservation trust and have returned to live in part of the house.

The original abbey was founded by the Cistercians in 1154. Fragments of this period survive round the rear courtyard and in a fine early 14th-century gatehouse, a rare example of this form not in ruins. It guards the entrance to the drive beneath a giant cedar, the tree so tilted as if about to blow away at any moment.

The main west wing dominates the scene. It is a rectangular box begun by Francis Smith of Warwick in 1720 for the 3rd Lord Leigh after his return from the Grand Tour. This box stimulated Jane Austen to her description of Sotherton in *Mansfield Park*. In 1809, Humphry Repton produced a Red Book for the landscape, including the diversion of the River Avon to form a lake to reflect the great west façade. John Rennie built a classical bridge over it five years later. Gothic Revival stables and a riding school were added shortly afterwards. Stoneleigh was a complete aristocratic encampment.

Above The original drawing room at Stoneleigh became known as the Silk Drawing Room in 1850. The needlework chairs were bought for the room by the 3rd Lord Leigh – they were valued at £60 in an inventory of 1738. The decor originally included crimson velvet wall hangings and mohair curtains.

The fire in 1960 destroyed the upper part of Smith's wing, leaving it derelict for over twenty years. Today, a scheme suggested by the last-resort saviour of many country houses, Kit Martin, has turned most of the house into apartments. The state rooms have been reinstated and are accessible, although their commercial use appears to demand fitted cream carpets, a dire anachronism which is at least reversible.

More controversial was the trustees' decision to patch rather than restore completely Smith's 15-bay façade. The result is plain ugly. Smith's vertical emphasis of rhythmic pilasters seems to have contracted a skin disease, the most virulent case of 20th-century 'conserve as found' I have encountered. It may work for a jumbled medieval façade, but devastates a classical design that depends on precision of detail and surface and the casting of shadow. One day, the unrestored stones will presumably need replacing, so Stoneleigh will be forever faced with chequerboard.

The interior was, at the time of my visit, still searching for personality beyond that of corporate hospitality. The staircase hall is superb, rising to a balcony and Venetian arch. Its walls are adorned with panels, trophies and hunting scenes beneath a ceiling rich in swags and shells. The balusters are composed of three different designs to each tread, twisted, spiral and classical.

Of the other rooms, the grandest is the 1765 saloon. It is surrounded with free-standing and attached columns in scagliola. The plasterwork, especially the oval ceiling panel and doorways, is of

the highest quality. Reliefs depict the Labours of Hercules. On the wall is a portrait of Helene Leigh, 'buccaneer' American wife of the 3rd Lord Leigh (of the second creation), whose money helped save Stoneleigh during a previous crisis at the turn of the 20th century.

Of the other rooms, the drawing room is wood-panelled and has the Leigh unicorn even on its light switches. The library has been refurnished with Georgian tapestry chairs by William Gomm, rightly returned to the house by the government after being surrendered by the Leighs in lieu of tax. There is a Georgian chapel with a plaster ceiling. The detached Gothic stables have been beautifully restored; the 1820s stalls are in their original state, sadly without horses.

The old house looks out once more over Repton's lake and park of 1808. He explicitly sought 'the graceful and picturesque combinations which we admire in the works of the best painters such as Poussin and Claude Lorraine and the scenery of the graceful Watteau'. Mansion and lake cast echoes at each other, especially on the riverside terrace.

STRATFORD-UPON-AVON

Anne Hathaway's cottage

✦✦✦ The family home of Shakespeare's wife

Cottage Lane, Shottery, Stratford-upon-Avon; museum, open all year

This is the most famous cottage in England, if not in the world. Anne Hathaway was William Shakespeare's wife. The image of her birthplace has sheltered a million chocolates and taxed a million jigsaw-puzzlers. Never was so small a spot so desirable to world tourism. Yet visit it off season and you may still have it to yourself. Anne Hathaway's Cottage is a masterpiece of unobtrusive fame.

Will and Anne married when he was eighteen and she an 'old maid' of twenty-six. Hathaways continued to live in the house for another three centuries. Celebrity came early. Tennyson and Dickens were enthusiastic visitors and Mary Baker, occupant of the cottage for much of the 19th

'Never was **so small a spot so desirable** to world tourism.'

century, was a practised guide. The Shakespeare Birthplace Trust acquired it in 1892.

Even without these associations, the cottage would be a pretty place. A thick bonnet of thatch slopes low over timbered walls and small windows. Roses and shrubs crowd close, while a herb garden and orchard grace the distance. This is the England of which expatriates dream and which many re-created in suburban repose.

The smaller half of the cottage is very old, probably 15th century, while the higher extension at the rear is of the 17th century. The rooms are intended by the Birthplace Trust to convey the appearance of the cottage at the time of its purchase at the end of the 19th century. There is little sign of museumitis, not much evidence of bardolatry and many charming relics of the cottage's past, including early photographs.

There are flagstones in the hall and game hanging in the larder. Upstairs is a series of bedrooms with old rope beds, origin of the night-time bidding to 'sleep tight'. On show is a beautifully carved crib and a chair made of straw. If these rooms were so well furnished, the Hathaways must have been prosperous. Between the old and new parts are exposed cruck beams and wattle-and-daub infill.

Despite the care shown with the cottage itself, I counted no fewer than four shops carefully inserted in the outbuildings. Opposite is the small pond in which, of course, Ophelia drowned.

William Shakespeare
1564–1616

Shakespeare was born in Stratford-upon-Avon, the son of John Shakespeare and Mary Arden. He was baptized on April 26th, but his exact birth date is unknown – it is generally celebrated on April 23rd, St George's Day, which was also the day on which he died.

In 1582 Shakespeare married Anne Hathaway, with whom he was to have three children. Little is known of his life between 1585 and 1592, but it is assumed he spent these years establishing his career as an actor and playwright in London. Most of his 38 plays were written for the Lord Chamberlain's Men, a company of players based at the Globe Theatre. By 1597 Shakespeare was successful enough to buy New Place, the second largest house in Stratford. No work by him after 1613 survives and it is presumed that he retired to New Place after this date. He was buried in Holy Trinity church.

UPON-AVON
Shakespeare's birthplace

 The childhood home of Britain's bard

Henley Street, Stratford-upon-Avon; museum, open all year

We may scoff at the scale of the Shakespeare industry, but what is Stratford to do? Block the roads, put guards at the gates, and sell timed tickets on the M40? The town has been a tourist magnet since the 18th century and much has indeed become tacky and commercialized. Yet for all the hordes, Stratford has at least guarded its shrines. The Shakespeare Birthplace Trust, set up in 1847, owns five properties in and round the town. Their quest for authenticity is not easy but almost everywhere is tasteful and sincere.

Shakespeare was born, educated and married amid the Elizabethan Midlands bourgeoisie. To

their houses he returned in middle age and lived there for the last six years of his life until his death aged fifty-two in 1616. The houses are best visited in mid-winter, although they are never allowed to become overcrowded since all are small, domestic residences. Adapt them for crowds, and they would collapse.

The Birthplace itself stands somewhat uncomfortably on Henley Street. Entry is through a modern visitors' centre which has displays that would be inappropriate in the house itself, such as the Bard's study and school desk. The original house is reached across a garden planted with herbs and flowers mentioned in the plays. The house remained in Shakespeare descent to the 19th century, when it passed to the Trust. Sadly, the houses on either side were demolished lest they ever catch fire and destroy the main house. They should be rebuilt facsimile.

Shakespeare's father, John, was a glover and clothier. In the rear parlour is a spinning wheel and much cloth. Next door is the family hall, combining as kitchen and dining room with the table laid for a meal. Beyond is John Shakespeare's workroom, complete with dressed animal skins. The plays are full of references to the skinner's trade.

The upstairs bedrooms are charmingly furnished with objects and fabrics from 16th-century originals. Here is the holy of holies, Shakespeare's birth-room, called in a Victorian advertisement 'the truly heart-stirring relic of England's immortal bard'. Here is a crib and baby clothes. A small exhibition describes the story of the house as a visitor attraction, with no celebrity omitted.

Hall's croft

★★ Jacobean house that belonged to Shakespeare's son-in-law

Old Town, Stratford-upon-Avon; museum, open all year

John Hall married Shakespeare's eldest daughter, Susanna, and appears to have built and occupied this house in 1613. Three years later he moved to Shakespeare's own house at New Place, now destroyed. Hall's Croft is an example of a town house to which Shakespeare might have aspired as a boy, and to which he returned at the end of his life. Hall was a physician and wealthy. His work is well documented and the house is an early museum of 'general practice'. Almost all the furniture is of the period.

In the downstairs parlour hangs a Dutch painting by Claeissins of a 16th-century family saying grace before a meal, the boys to one side, the girls to the other. On the table is a large haunch of beef, symbol of prosperity. Also in the room is a peculiar luxury, a beautifully turned child's high chair. Next to the parlour is Hall's consulting room, with Dutch paintings of apothecaries. The wall cupboard and work table display jars, pestles and mortars and other medical equipment. Everything looks painful.

Upstairs the rooms are mostly arranged for sleeping. One contains a lavatory stool with hinged lid. Even the servant's bedroom, on the same floor, is well appointed. The garden supplied the raw material for many of Hall's more complex herbal concoctions; a doctor had also to be a botanist. It has been beautifully restored, with an arbour and herbaceous border as well as herb garden. Shakespeare was intrigued by medical science. Theses have been written on the medicine in his plays, assumed to derive from his friendship with Hall.

STRATFORD-

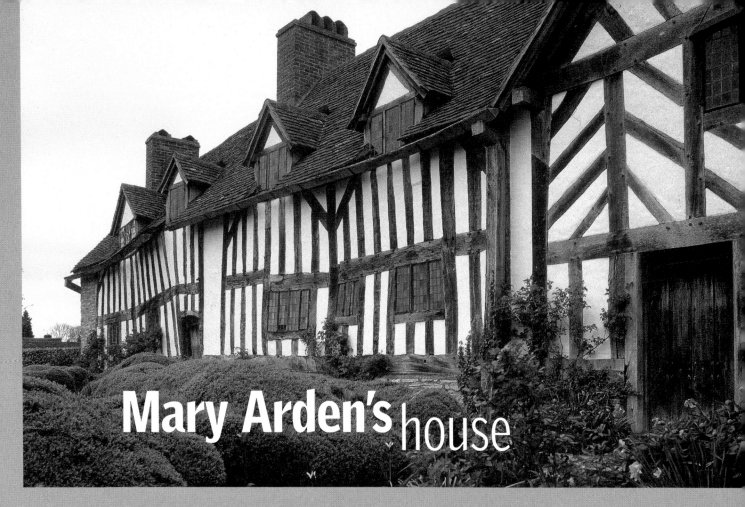

Mary Arden's house

⭐ The farmhouse home of Shakespeare's mother

Station Road, Wilmcote, Stratford-upon-Avon; museum, open all year

We have Shakespeare's birthplace, his wife's house, his daughter's house and his grand-daughter's house. Here, we even have his mother's family house, a substantial farm owned by the Arden family in the village of Wilmcote, north of the town. Recent research suggests that Glebe Farm, across a small meadow, may be the Arden house rather than the present building. The Shakespeare Birthplace Trust owns that as well. The holdings illustrate Shakespeare's rural roots alongside his upbringing as a tradesman's son. Mary Arden's House has been restored in Trust style, as picturesque as Anne Hathaway's Cottage. This is the Shakespeare of *As You Like It* and the Forest of Arden.

The first shock on passing the ticket desk is to encounter two live rams in a pen. This remains a farm. There are carts, calves, hayricks, a cider press and a dovecote, all listed in the will of Mary's father, Robert Arden. So too were the contents of the farmhouse, down to the pots, pans and furniture. They have been meticulously reinstated. The only anachronism in the living area is a Victorian mousetrap. The upstairs sleeping quarters were inserted at a later date into what had been a large open hall. The resulting attic beams offer a risk of banged heads.

In the Great Barn outside are further displays of Elizabethan and farmyard crafts. There is a working forge and falconry. Glebe Farm has now been restored and opened, and includes a late-Victorian laundry. It is all well done, the only omission being any dust, dirt or scruffiness. Perhaps they will come with time.

UPON-AVON

Nash's house

⭐ Elizabethan house that stood next-door to Shakespeare's now-lost house

Chapel Street, Stratford-upon-Avon; museum, open all year

Shakespeare would recognize Stratford's Chapel Street and Church Street. A Gothic church tower acts as the focus of a series of jettied upper storeys and timbered façades. On one side are the buildings of the Bard's old school. Beyond is the house occupied by Thomas Nash, who married Shakespeare's grand-daughter (see Abington Park, page 93). It is next to the site of New Place, where Shakespeare himself had a house for the last eighteen years of his life and where he died in 1616. The demolition and replacement of New Place in 1702, when its historic importance was already known, was a tragedy. The replacement was destroyed in 1759. We can only wander in the garden that marks its site.

New Place would have been similar to Nash's House. It is the most museum-like of the five Shakespeare houses, with pictures and furnishings of the period. On the ground floor, the hall, parlour and kitchen are emphatically

Dutch, reflecting close links between Britain and Holland at the turn of the 17th century. Porcelain and Flemish pictures line the walls. In the hall is a 'cupboard of boxes', a large 16th-century dresser. The kitchen is displayed as in the 19th century, reflecting the time when this part of the house was extended. (I note that museums require authenticity except when someone decides otherwise.)

The rooms upstairs contain a museum of Stratford history, including the first Shakespeare festival organized in the town by the actor David Garrick, in 1769. Outside, the knot garden is based on Elizabethan books and features plants mentioned in Shakespeare's plays. Beyond a pergola on the site of Shakespeare's old house is the Great Garden, flanked by an extraordinary yew hedge fronting the road. It is a series of trees shaped like gun batteries, with box hedges behind as ammunition. Who, other than tourists, is the enemy?

... the Upton collection is a model of personal connoisseurship ...

Upton house

✫✫ William-and-Mary house rebuilt for an art collection

7 miles NW of Banbury; National Trust, open part year

The first Viscount Bearsted was the son of an East End importer of decorative sea shells. He founded an oil company, which he named after his father's passion. His son in turn acquired an estate in Warwickshire and extended it in 1927 by buying a William-and-Mary hunting box at Upton.

Bearsted devoted himself not only to chairing his father's company but to amassing a huge art collection. Worried that punitive postwar taxation might lead to the break up of his collection, he gave it to the National Trust in 1948, heavily endowed. The condition was that his descendants be granted a perpetual tenancy. Samuels lived in the house until 1988 and the family still owns most of the estate, where they have a new house.

Upton is visited to see its paintings, porcelain and gardens, not architecture. Its 1920s interior is of the sort favoured by the international super-rich. Even the National Trust guidebook awards it 'the impersonality of a hotel or a liner'. Most of the rooms constitute a furnished art gallery, attended by a well-meaning but bossy staff. The pictures are unlabelled (as if in a private house) but numbered at random and not listed in numerical order in the catalogue, rendering it near unusable. Any attempt to retrace one's steps to see a missed painting is stopped by guards.

Above When Upton House was adapted in 1927 into a home for Walter Samuel, the 2nd Viscount Bearsted, three small rooms were transformed into a Long Gallery. Today the room is home to a collection of Dutch old masters, including paintings by Melchior de Hondecoeter and Jan Steen, and a selection of 18th-century English furniture.

Yet the Upton collection is a model of personal connoisseurship, one of those miniature 'national galleries' which abound in English houses. The entrance hall is hung with four Brussels tapestries. The first of the display rooms, the dining room, contains three Stubbs masterpieces, *The Haymakers*, *The Labourers* and *The Reapers*, majestic tributes to the dignity of work. The Long Gallery contains Dutch masters, including some charming Jan Steens. Cases of porcelain are predominantly of Chelsea.

The Picture Room gathers together historical English portraits by Reynolds and Raeburn and a Romney of William Beckford. Here hang two Hogarths for his print series of *The Four Times of Day*. The separate Picture Gallery, converted from a new squash court in the 1930s, displays works by Memling, van der Weyden, El Greco, Tintoretto and Hieronymous Bosch, the more enjoyable for being little known.

The gardens at Upton are, for Warwickshire, unusual. The lawn stretching away from the south front falls to what looks like a ha-ha, with a sheep-clad hillside in the distance. On closer inspection, it is not a ha-ha but a deep ravine. Terraces and herbaceous borders, avenues and ponds stretch over a mile into the distance. The National Trust's new restaurant in a handsome neo-classical style by Jeffrey Haworth is boldly sited as a garden feature.

Warwick castle

★★★★ An impressively grand castle with interiors that re-create historic eras

Castle Lane, Warwick; private house, open all year

Everything about Warwick is spectacular – the setting, the old town, the church, the high street and, above all, the castle. The last has seen every touch, turn and treachery of English history. When the hereditary custodians, the Brooke family, mercifully sold the place to Madame Tussaud's in 1978 and vanished overseas, the place at last came into its own.

Visiting Warwick Castle is a major (and costly) undertaking. Tussaud's run it as a business. They get no grant and give no quarter to critics of theme-park presentation. The castle is displayed round three periods, the Middle Ages, a 17th-century palace of state and a Victorian aristocratic residence. All are excellently done and Warwick is a delight to visit. It is a model of how hundreds of similar houses must adapt when they are no longer residences but must attract the public as customers rather than supplicants. If a house cannot be a home, at least let it pack a punch as Warwick does.

The original castle of William the Conqueror survives on a mound behind the existing one. The surrounding bailey was progressively fortified in the 12th and 13th centuries. But it was the arrival of the Beauchamps in 1268 that produced the present romantic composition, of towers, halls and curtain walls. The Beauchamps, first alone and then through marriage to the Nevilles, embodied the might of baronial England. They fought, schemed, married, built and fought again. Then they built some more.

WARWICK

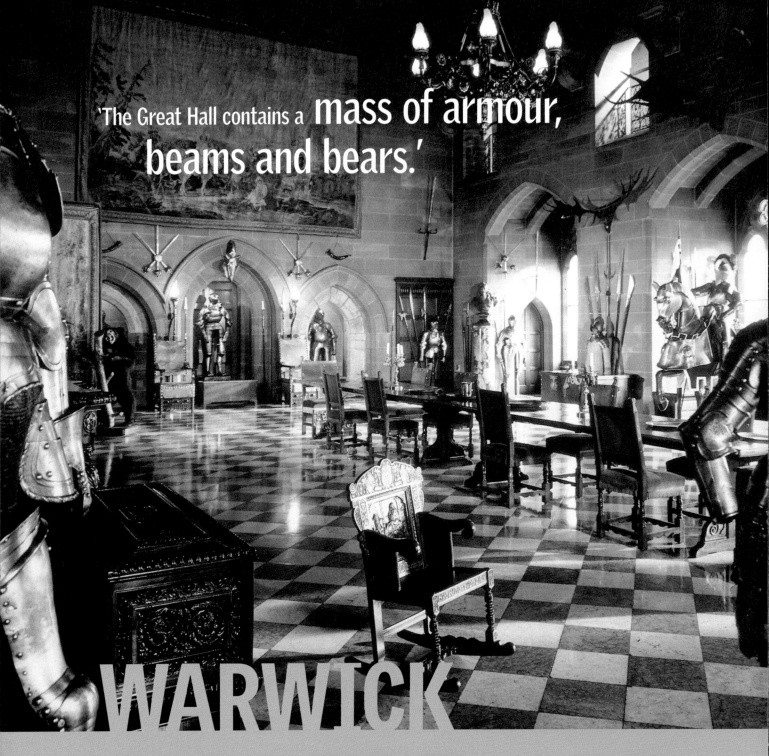

'The Great Hall contains a **mass of armour, beams and bears.'**

WARWICK

The last of the line, the 'Kingmaker' Richard Neville, deposed two kings during the Wars of the Roses before falling to the Yorkists at the Battle of Barnet in 1471. After his death, the castle was seized and held by the Crown, until James I awarded it to the Fulke Grevilles, later Barons Brooke; they regained the title of Earls of Warwick in the 18th century.

The castle's outer wall shuts it away from the town along its entire length. Once inside the grounds, however, we see the work of centuries. Most magnificent is the view from the River Avon below, of the main façade and Caesar's Tower. Here Warwick is presented as a textbook of military-cum-residential architecture, on a par with Windsor, Arundel and Raby castles. While it is hard to tell medieval from Victorian restoration, I am inclined to answer, so what? From the 14th century to the 19th the English have regarded castellation as the true sign of ancestral dignity.

The interior is approached through the inner bailey. The castle today presents itself in three distinct guises. First, we see it enmeshed in the Wars of the Roses on the eve of battle. The torture chamber and dungeon of death or glory are accompanied with armouries, smithies, stables and fond farewells. These are the best tableau re-creations of medieval England that I know. Elsewhere in the bailey are lesser keeps, turrets, ramparts and a haunted tower. The last is furnished in the Jacobean style of its restorer, Sir Fulke Greville, who was killed in an argument over money with a servant. In his room is a magnificent Jacobean bed. His ghost is said still to haunt the tower.

The residential castle begins with the chapel and state dining room. In the latter hangs one of five van Dyck depictions of Charles I on a horse. The Great Hall contains a mass of armour, beams and bears. Here too is the celebrated Kenilworth Buffet, covered in Victorian carving depicting Elizabeth I's arrival in splendour at Kenilworth Castle to be entertained by her admirer, Dudley.

Left The Great Hall displays the trappings of military might. A Beauvais tapestry depicting the Duke of Marlborough's army on the march hangs on the east wall. **Below** The library is furnished as it was during a weekend party in 1898 and peopled with waxwork figures of actual guests. In front of the fire stands the Countess of Warwick and Winston Churchill, holding a book; seated on the sofa is the Duke of Devonshire.

Above In the ladies' boudoir is a waxwork of Millicent, Duchess of Sutherland; her half-sister Daisy was the Countess of Warwick and hostess of the 1898 weekend party now re-created in the former private apartments, using old photographs as a guide. The guest list for that weekend included the Prince of Wales, later Edward VII.

There follows a sumptuous suite of Stuart and Georgian reception rooms, named Red, Cedar and Green. Queen Anne's bedroom was furnished for a visit in 1704 which never occurred. She was dreadful at keeping these dates. The tapestries depict royal gardens; their colours were fixed with urine, a workman being paid to drink quantities of beer to maintain supplies.

Finally comes Warwick's tableau of an Edwardian 'royal weekend party', based on a genuine 1898 guest list. Guests preparing for dinner included the Prince of Wales, Lord Curzon, Winston Churchill, the Dukes of Devonshire and Marlborough and their ladies. The characters are depicted in Tussaud's finest wax, gossiping, dressing, singing, smoking and having their hair prepared for dinner. A maid even fills a bath (with real water). This is done with admirable realism, as close to life as artifice allows. If wax we must have, let it be Tussaud's wax.

The Lord Leycester hospital

★★ Surviving premises of medieval guilds

High Street, Warwick; museum, open all year

The Lord Leycester Hospital lies over the West Gate into Warwick beneath the outer walls of the castle. It was home to the pre-Reformation United Guilds of Warwick, a group of societies which worshipped in the old chantry chapel of St James above the gate and met in buildings flanking the street. After the Dissolution, Robert Dudley, Earl of Leicester, sought a home for his pensioner soldiers and their wives, and acquired the guild premises. In 1571 they were assigned to a Master and twelve resident Brethren.

Thus they have remained ever since, with only a mild adjustment to the governance and a reduction from twelve brethren to eight. They support themselves by keeping the place in order and selling tickets to tourists. They must worship every day in the chapel, where each has a stall.

The ensemble is picturesque and often in use as a film set. The courtyard is surrounded by the old guild hall, the Great Hall, the kitchen and the Master's house. The last is a colourful Victorian veneer on what was an unstable timbered wall, now painted to look original. The heraldic emblems are added for antique effect: the Bear and Ragged Staff is the emblem of Dudley and the Porcupine of his descendants, the Sidneys. The Great Hall dates from the 1380s, with a magnificent queen-post roof. The plastic chairs are a pity.

The hall in which the guilds met is later, c1450, but smaller and more barnlike, with collar-beams and plaster walls. It forms part of a regimental museum. Back in the courtyard is the brethren's kitchen where the inmates ate collectively until given self-contained flats in the 1960s. The room is now a cafeteria where tourists eat under the motto 'droit et loyal'.

Glossary

The aim in this book has been to avoid terms not familiar to the lay person. However, some specialist terms in common use in architectural circles may have crept in, for which the following may be helpful.

acanthus – pattern of an exotic Mediterranean flower with large leaves used in classical decoration.

anthemion – a honeysuckle flower pattern used in classical decoration.

Artisan Mannerist – buildings created by masons using pattern books (rather than architects) in the period c.1615–75. Mannerism originated in 16th-century Italy and was characterised by Classical elements used in unusual ways. It was taken up in the Low Countries, then spread to England.

ashlar – block of masonry fashioned into a wall, either load-bearing or to cover brick.

bailey, inner and outer – a fortified enclosure, usually moated and surrounded by a curtain wall, containing a motte (mound) with a keep on top. Walls are topped by battlements, with crenellations which protected defenders from arrows, and machicolations, or floor openings, through which attackers could be fired down on.

baluster – upright post supporting the handrail on stairs.

bargeboard – wooden board protecting the eaves of a roof.

bay – a space of wall between any vertical element, such as an upright beam, pillar or a division into a window or door.

bay window – window projecting out from a flat wall, either canted if the sides are straight, or bowed if curved.

bolection mould – moulding concealing the join of vertical and horizontal surfaces, shaped like an S in cross-section.

Boulle – elaborate inlay work on the surface of furniture, customary in 17th and 18th-century French work.

bow – see bay window

canted – see bay window

cartouche – frame for a picture or statue, often oval and surrounded by a scroll.

caryatid – a column in the shape of a draped female figure.

casements – see sashes

castle of enclosure – a form of early medieval castle in which individual buildings are enclosed within a curtain wall, in contrast to later medieval castles that consisted of a tower with subsidiary buildings in a courtyard to front or rear.

chinoiserie – a style of Rococo with Chinese motifs, often linked with Gothick.

coffering – a ceiling composed of beams enclosing sunken square or round panels.

collars – see roof timbers

corbel – a stone or wood projection in a wall that supports a beam, statue or sill.

cornice – (1) a ledge or projecting upper part of a classical entablature. (2) Moulding at the top of a wall concealing the join with the ceiling.

cottage ornée – late-Georgian/Victorian picturesque cottage, usually with thatched roof and Gothic windows.

crenellation – see bailey

crocket – Gothic decorative device, usually a cusp or curling leaf, at regular intervals on outer edges of spires, pinnacles and gables

cruck – a simple structure of two, usually curved, trunks of wood formed into an inverted V which support the walls and roof of a medieval house.

curtain wall – in castle-building, a wall constructed between defensive projections such as bastions.

dentil – one of a series of small square blocks along the base of a cornice

dorter – a sleeping room or dormitory, especially in a college or monastery.

dressing – a general term for finishings; stone is dressed to either a smooth or ornamental surface.

enfilade – a line of rooms in sequence along one side of a house, usually with interconnecting doors.

entablature – a feature of classical architecture comprising everything above column height, formally composed of architrave, frieze and cornice.

flatwork – decorative plaster or woodwork in low relief.

frontispiece – a decorative bay above a doorway in a Tudor or Jacobean building, customarily composed of Renaissance motifs.

gable – the triangular end of a double-pitched roof, sometimes with stepped or scrolled (Dutch) sides.

garderobe – privy or lavatory, usually discharging into a ditch or moat outside a medieval house.

Great Chamber – see solar

grisaille – monochrome painting, usually a mural and in shades of grey.

grotesque – decorative wall motif of human figures, as found in Roman grottoes.

half-timbering – term for timber-framed house derived from the practice of splitting logs in half to provide beams.

hipped roof – a roof with a sloping end instead of an end gable.

Ho-Ho bird – chinoiserie motif associated with 18th-century Rococo style.

jetty or jettied floor – upper floor extended, or oversailed, beyond the lower one to give more space upstairs and protect lower walls from adverse weather. Jettying also uses the downward thrust of the upper walls to form a cantilever, preventing internal ceiling beams from bowing.

keep – see bailey

king post – see roof timbers

linenfold – a pattern on wall panels imitating folded linen.

louvre – a covered turret above a medieval hall that allowed smoke to escape.

machicolation – see bailey

mannerism – see Artisan Mannerist

mansard – a roof with two separate pitches of slope.

motte – see bailey

mullion – central divider of window, made of metal or stone.

oversail – see jetty

oriel – an upper window projecting from a wall, sometimes (incorrectly) used to indicate a tall medieval window lighting the dais end of the Great Hall.

Palladian – a style of classical architecture, formal and refined outside, often lavish inside, named after Italian architect, Andrea Palladio (1508–80). Moving spirit behind most English classical designers, especially Inigo Jones and, later, Lord Burlington, William Kent and the early Georgians.

parlour – see solar

piano nobile – the main ceremonial floor of a classical building, sitting on the basement or 'rustic' lower floor.

pier-glass – a wall mirror supported by a small table, bracket or console.

pietra dura – literally 'hard stone'; a decorative inlay using highly polished stones such as marble, jasper and porphyry

pilaster – a flat column projecting only slightly from a wall.

pointing – mortar or cement used to seal between bricks.

porte-cochère – a grand porch with a driveway through it, allowing passengers to alight from carriages under cover.

prodigy house – a large, ostentatious house of the Elizabethan/Jacobean period.

putti – unwinged sculptures of chubby boys found in Classical and Baroque decoration.

queen post – see roof timbers

quoins – dressed corner stones.

render – a covering of stucco, cement or limewash on the outside of a building.

Rococo – the final phase of Baroque style in the 18th century, typified by refined painted and plaster decoration, often asymmetrical and with figures.

roof timbers – a tie-beam runs horizontally across the roof space; a king post rises vertically from the tie beam to the apex of the roof; queen posts rise not to the apex but to subsidiary beams known as collars; wind-braces strengthen the roof rafters.

rustic – a name given in Palladian architecture to the lower floor or basement, beneath the piano nobile.

rustication – treatment of ashlar by deep-cutting joints so they look stronger or cruder.

sashes – windows opening by rising on sash ropes or cords, as opposed to casements which open on side hinges.

scagliola – composition of artificial stone that imitates appearance of grained marble.

screens passage – accessed from the main door of a medieval building and built into one end of a Great Hall to shield it from draughts. Door ors arches lead from the passage into the hall on one side and kitchens on other. Above is usually a minstrels' gallery.

Serlian – motifs derived from pattern books of the Italian Renaissance architect, Sebastiano Serlio (1475–1554).

sgraffito – plaster decoration scratched to reveal another colour beneath.

solar – the upstairs room at the family end of a medieval hall, originally above an undercroft or parlour. Originally accessed by ladder or spiral stairs, it was usually replaced by a Great Chamber in the Tudor era.

strapwork – strap or ribbon-like decorative scrolls in Elizabethan and Jacobean design.

stucco – plaster, usually protective, covering for brick, sometimes fashioned to look like stone.

studding – vertical timbers laid close to each other to strengthen the wall. Close-studding tends to indicate wealth.

tie-beam – see roof timbers

undercroft – a vaulted room or crypt beneath a building, partly or wholly underground

vault – a ceiling, usually of stone composed of arches.

Venetian window – Palladian window composed of three components, the centre one arched.

wind-braces – see roof timbers

Simon Jenkins' sources

The best guides to any house are the people who occupy it. They have felt its walls and sensed its seasons. They stand witness to its ghosts, real and imagined, and have thus become part of its history. As a substitute, guidebooks vary widely from the academic to the plain childish. The best are published by English Heritage, erudite and enjoyable. National Trust guidebooks are at last moving from the scholarly to the accessible, and the Trust's compendium *Guide*, by Lydia Greeves and Michael Trinick, is excellent.

My selection of a thousand properties derives from numerous sources. These include Hudson's *Historic Houses and Gardens*, supplemented by *Museums and Galleries* published by Tomorrow's Guides. The Historic Houses Association website is another invaluable source. Of recent house surveys, the best are John Julius Norwich's *Architecture of Southern England* (1985), John Martin Robinson's *Architecture of Northern England* (1986) and Hugh Montgomery-Massingberd's *Great Houses of England and Wales* (2000). Nigel Nicolson's *Great Houses of Britain* (1978) describes the most prominent. Their lists are not exhaustive and include houses not open to the public. Behind them stands Nikolaus Pevsner's massive 'Buildings of England' series, which deals with houses more generously (with plans) in the newer revised editions.

On English domestic architecture, the classics are hard to beat. They include Olive Cook's *The English House Through Seven Centuries* (1968), Alec Clifton-Taylor's *The Pattern of English Building* (1972), Hugh Braun's *Old English Houses* (1962), Sacheverell Sitwell's *British Architects and Craftsmen* (1964) and Plantagenet Somerset Fry's *Castles of Britain and Ireland* (1980).

On specific periods the best are Mark Girouard's *Robert Smythson and the English Country House* (1983), Giles Worsley's *Classical Architecture in England* (1995), Kerry Downes's *English Baroque Architecture* (1966) and Girouard's *The Victorian Country House* (1971). Joe Mordaunt Crook takes a lively look at the Victorian battle of the styles in *The Dilemma of Style* (1989). Jeremy Musson describes the manorial revival in *The English Manor House* (1999) and Gavin Stamp takes a wider look at the same period in *The English House 1860–1914* (1986). *Edwardian Architecture*, edited by Alastair Service (1975), brings the story into the 20th century and Clive Aslet's *The Last Country Houses* (1982) almost completes it.

On social history, Girouard's *Life in the English Country House* (1978) is incomparable. *Creating Paradise* (2000) by Richard Wilson and Alan Mackley sets the house in its economic context. So does Mordaunt Crook's *The Rise of the Nouveaux Riches* (1999) and David Cannadine's *The Decline and Fall of the British Aristocracy* (1990). Adrian Tinniswood offers a fascinating insight in his *History of Country House Visiting* (1989). The desperate post-war bid to save houses is described in Marcus Binney's *Our Vanishing Heritage* (1984) and John Cornforth's *The Country Houses of England 1948–1998* (1998). Peter Mandler covers the same period in his scholarly *The Fall and Rise of the Stately Home* (1997).

Biographies of architects are too legion to list but Howard Colvin's *Biographical Dictionary of British Architects* (1978) was my bible over disputed dates and attributions. Of a more personal character is James Lees-Milne's delightful account of the National Trust's early acquisitions in *People and Places* (1992). Houses in distress are visited in John Harris's *No Voice from the Hall* (1998). *Writers and their Houses* (1993) is a first-class collection of essays, edited by Kate Marsh.

I am indebted to the many architectural commentaries in *Country Life*, champion of the historic buildings cause for over a century. I do not believe I could have found a thousand houses for my list were it not for its progenitors, Edward Hudson and Christopher Hussey, and their many successors.

Contact details

Note: Readers are advised to check opening times before visiting, either via the websites and addresses below or in Hudson's Historic Houses & Gardens, the annual guide to castles, houses and heritage sites open to the public. Houses sited close to the border of a neighbouring county may have that county given as their postal address.

Althorp – Althorp, Northamptonshire, NN7 4HQ www.althorp.com Tel 01604 770107 Open early Jul–late Aug, daily 11am–5pm

Arbury Hall – Nuneaton, Warwickshire, CV10 7PT Tel 024 7638 2804 Open Easter–Sep, BH Suns & BH Mons 2–5pm

Ashby de la Zouch Castle – South Street, Ashby de la Zouch, Leicestershire, LE65 1BR www.english-heritage.org.uk/ashbydelazouch Tel 01530 413343 Open all year, Thur–Mon (daily in Jul–Aug) 10am–5pm (to 6pm in Jul–Aug, to 4pm in Nov–Mar)

Aubourn Hall – Lincoln, Lincolnshire, LN5 9DZ Tel 01522 788199 Grounds open by arrangement

Baddesley Clinton – Rising Lane, Baddesley Clinton Village, Knowle, Solihull, West Midlands, B93 0DQ www.nationaltrust.org.uk Tel 01564 783294 Open early Feb–early Nov, Wed–Sun 11am–5pm

Belton House – Grantham, Lincolnshire, NG32 2LS www.nationaltrust.org.uk Tel 01476 566116 Open early Mar–early Nov, Wed–Sun (Sat–Sun in early– mid-Mar) 12.30–5pm (to 4pm in early–mid-Mar)

Belvoir Castle – Belvoir, Leicestershire, NG32 1PE www.belvoircastle.com Tel 01476 871003 Open Easter & May–Sep, Sat–Thur (daily during Easter holidays, closed Mon in May–Jun, Sat–Sun only in Sep) 11am–5pm (to 4pm on Sat)

Birmingham: Aston Hall – Trinity Road, Aston, Birmingham, B6 6JD www.bmag.org.uk Tel 0121 327 0062 Open Apr–Oct, Tue–Sun & BH Mon 11.30am–4pm

Birmingham: Blakesley Hall – Blakesley Road, Yardley, Birmingham, B25 8RN www.bmag.org.uk Tel 0121 464 2193 Open late Mar–late Oct, Tue–Sun & BH Mon 11.30am–4pm

Birmingham: Selly Manor – Maple Road, Bournville, Birmingham, B30 2AE www.bvt.org.uk/sellymanor Tel 0121 472 0199 Open all year, Tue–Fri 10am–5pm (also Sat–Sun & BH Mon 2–5pm in Apr–Sep)

Birmingham: Soho House – Soho Avenue (off Soho Road), Handsworth, Birmingham, B18 5LB www.bmag.org.uk Tel 0121 554 9122 Open late Mar–late Oct, Tue–Sun & BH Mon 11.30am–4pm

Boughton House – Kettering, Northamptonshire, NN14 1BJ www.boughtonhouse.org.uk Tel 01536 515731 Open early Aug–early Sep, daily 2–5pm

Canons Ashby – Canons Ashby, Daventry, Northamptonshire, NN11 3SD www.nationaltrust.org.uk Tel 01327 861900 Open early Mar–mid-Dec, Sat–Wed (Sat–Sun in early–mid-Mar & early–mid-Dec) 1–5pm (to 4pm in early Oct–mid-Dec, from 12pm in early–mid-Dec)

Charlecote Park – Warwick, CV35 9ER www.nationaltrust.org.uk Tel 01789 470277 Open early Mar–late Oct, Fri–Tue 12–5pm (also open weekends in early–late-Dec, 12–4pm)

Coombe Abbey Hotel – Brinklow Road, Binley, Coventry, CV3 2AB www.coombeabbey.com Tel 024 7645 0450

Cottesbrooke Hall – Cottesbrooke, Northamptonshire, NN6 8PF www.cottesbrookehall.co.uk Tel 01604 505808 Open May–Sep, Thur & BH Mon (also Wed in May–Jun) 2–5.30pm

Coughton Court – Nr Alcester, Warwickshire, B49 5JA www.nationaltrust.org.uk Tel 01789 400777 Open mid-Mar–late Sep, Wed–Sun (also open Tue in Jul–Aug) 11am–5pm (also open weekends in early Oct–early Nov)

Deene Park – Corby, Northamptonshire, NN17 3EW www.deenepark.com Tel 01780 450278 Open Jun–Aug, Sun (also Easter Sun & Mon, Aug BH Mon) 2–5pm

Doddington Hall – Doddington, Lincoln, Lincolnshire, LN6 4RU www.doddingtonhall.com Tel 01522 694308 Open May–Sep, We, Sun & BH Mon 1–5pm

Donnington-le-Heath Manor House – Manor Road, Donnington-le-Heath, Leicestershire, LE67 2FW Tel 01530 831259/0116 265 8326 Open all year, daily (Sat–Sun in Dec–Feb, although may be open some weekdays, contact for information) 11am–4pm

Eastwood: D. H. Lawrence House – 8a Victoria Street, Eastwood, Nottinghamshire, NG16 3AW www.broxtowe.gov.uk Tel 0177 371 7353 Open all year, daily 10am–5pm (to 4pm in Nov–Mar)

Epworth: The Old Rectory – 1 Rectory Street, Epworth, Lincolnshire, DN9 1HX www.epwortholdrectory.org.uk Tel 01427 872268 Open Mar–Oct, daily 10am–12pm & 2–4pm (2–4pm on Sun & Good Fri, to 4.30pm in May–Sep)

Ettington Park Hotel – Alderminster, Stratford-upon-Avon, Warwickshire, CV37 8BU Tel 0845 072 7454

Farnborough Hall – Farnborough, Banbury, Oxfordshire, OX17 1DU www.nationaltrust.org.uk Tel 01295 690002 Open early Apr–late Sep, Wed & Sat (also May BH Sun & Mon) 2–5.30pm

Fawsley Hall Hotel – Fawsley, Nr Daventry, Northamptonshire, NN11 3BA www.fawsleyhall.com Tel 01327 892000

Gainsborough Old Hall – Parnell Street, Gainsborough, Lincolnshire, DN21 2NB www.english-heritage.org.uk/gainsborough Tel 01427 612669 Open all year, daily (Mon–Sat in Nov–Mar) 10am–5pm (1–4.30pm on Sun)

Grimsthorpe Castle – Grimsthorpe, Bourne, Lincolnshire, PE10 0LY www.grimsthorpe.co.uk Tel 01778 591205 Open Apr–Sep, Sun, Thur & BH Mon (Sun–Thur in Aug) 1–4.30pm

Gunby Hall – Gunby, Nr Spilsby, Lincolnshire, PE23 5SS www.nationaltrust.org.uk Tel 07870 758876 Open early Jun–late Aug, Wed 2–5pm

Harlaxton Manor – Harlaxton College, Grantham, Lincolnshire, NG32 1AG www.ueharlax.ac.uk Tel 01476 403000 Open for pre-booked tours, contact the Library on 01476 403024

Holdenby House – Holdenby, Northamptonshire, NN6 8DJ www.holdenby.com Tel 01604 770074 Open on certain days only, contact for information; gardens open Apr & Sep, Sun 1–5pm

Holme Pierrepont Hall – Holme Pierrepont, Nr Nottingham, Nottinghamshire, NG12 2LD www.holmepierreponthall.com Tel 0115 933 22371 Open early Feb–mid-Mar, Mon–Wed 2–5pm (also open some Suns in Feb–Apr)

Honington Hall – Shipston-on-Stour, Warwickshire, CV36 5AA. Tel 01608 661434 Open by appointment

Kelham Hall – Kelham, Newark, Nottinghamshire, NG23 5QX Contact Newark & Sherwood District Council on 01636 650000 for access information

Kelmarsh Hall – Kelmarsh, Northamptonshire, NN6 9LT www.kelmarsh.com Tel 01604 686543 Open May–Sep, Thur & BH Sun & Mon (also Easter Sun & Mon) 2–5pm

Kenilworth Castle – Kenilworth, Warwickshire, CV8 1NE www.english-heritage.org.uk/kenilworth Tel 01926 864152 Open all year, daily 10am–5pm (to 6pm in Jul–Aug & to 4pm in Nov–Feb)

Kirby Hall – Deene, Corby, Northamptonshire, NN17 3EN www.english-heritage.org.uk/kirbyhall Tel 01536 203230 Open all year, Thur–Mon (daily in Jul–Aug) 10am–5pm (to 6pm in Jul–Aug & 11am–3pm in Nov–Mar)

Kirby Muxloe Castle – Kirby Muxloe, Leicestershire, LE9 9MD www.english-heritage.org.uk/kirbymuxloe Tel 0116 238 6886 Open Jul–Aug, Sat–Sun 10am–5pm

Lamport Hall – Lamport, Northamptonshire, NN6 9HD www.lamporthall.co.uk Tel 01604 686272 Open early Apr–mid-Oct, Sun (Mon–Fri in Aug) for guided tours

Leicester: Belgrave Hall – Church Road, off Thurcaston Road, Belgrave, Leicester, Leicestershire, LE4 5PE www.leicestermuseums.ac.uk Tel 0116 266 6590 Open Feb–Oct, Sun–Wed 11am–4.30pm (from 1pm on Sun)

Leicester: Newarke Houses – The Newarke, Leicester, Leicestershire, LE2 7BY www.leicestermuseums.ac.uk Tel 0116 225 4980 Open all year, daily 10am–5pm (from 11am on Sun)

Lincoln: Jew's House – 15 The Strait & 1 Steep Hill, Lincoln, Lincolnshire, LN2 1JD www.jewshouserestaurant.co.uk Tel 01522 524851

Lyddington Bede House – Blue Coat Lane, Luddington, Uppingham, Rutland, LE15 9LZ www.english-heritage.org.uk/lyddington Tel 01572 822438 Open Apr–Oct, Thur–Mon 10am–5pm

Lyveden New Bield – Nr Oundle, Peterborough, PE8 5AT www.nationaltrust.org.uk Tel 01832 205358 Open late Mar–late Oct, Wed–Sun, BH Mon & Good Fri (daily in Aug) 10.30am–5pm; also weekends in Nov & Feb–Mar

Marston Hall – Marston, Grantham, Lincolnshire, NG32 2HQ Tel 07812 356237 Open on various weekends throughout the year, contact for further details

Middleton Hall – Middleton, Tamworth, Staffordshire, B78 2AE Tel 01827 283095 Open Eater–late Sep, Sun & BH Mon 2–5pm (from 11am on BH Mon)

Nassington: Prebendal Manor House – Nassington, Peterborough, PE8 6QG www.prebendal-manor.co.uk Tel 01780 782575 Open Easter & Apr–Sep, Sun (also Wed & BH Mon in May–Sep) 2–5pm

Newark Castle – Castlegate, Newark-on-Trent, Nottinghamshire, NG24 1BZ Tel 01636 655765 (Tourist Information Centre) Grounds open all year, daily, dawn to dusk; guided tours available

Newstead Abbey – Newstead Abbey Park, Nottinghamshire, NG15 8NA www.newsteadabbey.org.uk Tel 01623 455900 Open Apr–Sep, daily 12–5pm; grounds open all year, daily 9am–6pm or dusk if earlier

Normanby Hall – Normanby, Scunthorpe, Lincolnshire, DN15 9HU www.northlincs.gov.uk/normanby Tel 01724 720588 Open Apr–Sep, daily 1–5pm

Northampton: Abington Park – Park Avenue South, Northampton, Northamptonshire, NN1 5LW www.northampton.gov.uk Tel 01604 838110 Open all year, Tue–Sun & BH Mon 1–5pm (to 4pm on Tue–Sun in Nov–Feb)

Nottingham: Brewhouse Yard – Castle Boulevard, Nottingham, Nottinghamshire, NG7 1FB www.nottinghamcity.gov.uk Tel 0115 915 3600 Open all year, daily 10am–4.30pm

Nottingham: Wollaton Hall – Wollaton, Nottingham, Nottinghamshire, NG8 2AE www.nottinghamcity.gov.uk Tel 0115 915 3900 Open all year, daily 11am–4pm

Nottingham: Ye Olde Salutation Inn – Houndsgate, Maid Marion Way, Nottingham, Nottinghamshire, NG1 7AA Tel 0115 958 9432

Oakham Castle – Castle Lane, off Market Place, Oakham, Rutland, LE15 6DF www.rutnet.co.uk/rcccastle Tel 01572 758440 Open all year, daily 10.30am–1pm & 1.30–5pm (2–4pm on Sun)

Packwood House – Lapworth, Solihull, West Midlands, B94 6AT www.nationaltrust.org.uk Tel 01564 783294 Open early Feb–early Nov, Wed–Sun 11am–5pm

Papplewick Hall – Papplewick, Nottinghamshire, NG15 8FE Tel 0115 963 3491 Open by appointment on 1st, 3rd & 5th Wed in every month, 2–5pm

Ragley Hall – Alcester, Warwickshire, B49 5NJ www.ragleyhall.com Tel 01789 762090 Open late Mar–late Sep, Thur–Sun & BH Mon 11am–4pm (to 1pm on Sat)

Rockingham Castle – Rockingham, Market Harborough, Leicestershire, LE16 8TH www.rockinghamcastle.com Tel 01536 770240 Open Easter–Sep, Sun & BH Mon (also Tue in Jun–Sep) 1–4.30pm

Rushton Triangular Lodge – Rushton, Kettering, Northamptonshire, NN14 1RP www.english-heritage.org.uk/rushton Tel 01536 710761 Open Apr–Oct, Thur–Mon 11am–4pm

Southwell: Workhouse – Upton Road, Southwell, Nottinghamshire, NG25 0PT www.nationaltrust.org.uk Tel 01636 817250 Open early Mar–early Nov, Sat–Sun (also Wed–Fri mid-Mar–late Sep) 11am–4pm (12–5pm in Apr–Sep)

Southwick Hall – Southwick, Nr Oundle, Peterborough, PE8 5BL www.southwickhall.co.uk Tel 01832 274064 Open Easter–Aug, BH Suns & BH Mons 2–5pm

Spalding: Ayscoughfee Hall – Churchgate, Spalding, Lincolnshire, PE11 2RA www.ayscoughfee.org Tel 01775 764555 Open all year, Tue–Sun & BH Mon 10.30am–5pm (from 12 noon weekdays in winter, to 7pm on Thur in summer, 9.30–4pm on Sat–Sun)

Stanford Hall – Lutterworth, Leicestershire, LE17 6DH www.stanfordhall.co.uk Tel 01788 860250 Open mid-Apr–late Sep, Sun & BH Mon (not Aug BH Mon) 1.30–5.30pm

Stapleford Park Hotel – Stapleford, Nr Melton Mowbray, Leicestershire, LE14 2EF www.staplefordpark.com Tel 01572 787000

Staunton Harold Hall – Melbourne Road, Staunton Harold, Ashby de la Zouch, Leicestershire, LE65 1RT Tel 01332 862599 Open for tours by arrangement; grounds also open to the public

Stoke Park – Stoke Bruerne, Towcester, Northamptonshire, NN12 7RZ Tel 01604 862329 Open Aug, daily 3–6pm

Stoke Rochford Hall – Stoke Rochford, nr Grantham, Lincolnshire, NG33 5EJ www.stokerochfordhall.co.uk Tel 01476 530337 Now a residential conference centre, contact for access information

Stoneleigh Abbey – Kenilworth, Warwickshire, CV8 2LF www.stoneleighabbey.org Tel 01926 858535 Open Easter–late Oct, Tue–Thur, Sun, Good Fri & BHs for tours

Stratford: Anne Hathaway's Cottage – Cottage Lane, Shottery, Stratford-upon-Avon, Warwickshire, CV37 9HH www.shakespeare.org.uk Tel 01789 292100 Open all year, daily 9.30am–5pm (from 9am in Jun–Aug, times vary on Suns)

Stratford: Shakespeare's Birthplace – Henley Street, Stratford-upon-Avon, Warwickshire, CV37 6QW www.shakespeare.org.uk Tel 01789 204016 Open all year, daily 10am–5pm (from 9.30am in Jun–Aug, to 4pm in Nov–Mar, times vary on Suns)

Stratford: Hall's Croft – Old Town, Stratford-upon-Avon, Warwickshire, CV37 6BG www.shakespeare.org.uk Tel 01789 292107 Open all year, daily 11am–5pm (from 9.30am in Jun–Aug, to 4pm in Nov–Mar, times vary on Suns)

Stratford: Mary Arden's House – Station Road, Wilmcote, Stratford-upon-Avon Warwickshire, CV37 9UN www.shakespeare.org.uk Tel 01789 293455 Open all year, daily, 10am–5pm (from 9.30am in Jun–Aug, to 4pm in Nov–Mar)

Stratford: Nash's House – Chapel Street, Stratford-upon-Avon, Warwickshire, CV37 6EP www.shakespeare.org.uk Tel 01789 292 325 Open all year, daily, 11am–5pm (from 9.30am in Jun–Aug, to 4pm in Nov–Mar, times vary on Suns)

Sulgrave Manor – Manor Road, Sulgrave, Nr Banbury, Oxfordshire, OX17 2SD www.sulgravemanor.org.uk Tel 01295 760205 Open Apr–Oct, Sat–Sun (also Tue–Thur in May–Oct) 12–4pm (from 2pm on Tue–Thur)

Tattershall Castle – Tattershall, Lincoln, LN4 4LR www.nationaltrust.org.uk Tel 01526 3425443 Open early Mar–mid-Dec, Sat–Sun (Sat–Wed in mid-Mar–early Nov) 12–4pm (from 11am in mid-Mar–early Nov, to 5.30pm in mid-Mar–early Oct)

Thoresby Hall Hotel – Thoresby Park, Nr Ollerton, Nottinghamshire, NG22 9WH www.warnerbreaks.co.uk Tel 01623 821 000

Thrumpton Hall – Thrumpton, Nottinghamshire, NG11 0AX www.thrumptonhall.com Tel 0115 983 0410 Open by appointment

Upton Hall – Upton, Newark, Nottinghamshire, NG23 5TE www.bhi.co.uk Tel 01636 813795 Open by appointment

Upton House – Banbury, Oxfordshire, OX15 6HT www.nationaltrust.org.uk Tel 01295 670266 Open early Mar–late Dec, Sat–Wed (daily in mid–late Mar & late Jul–late Aug) 11am–5pm (12–4pm in early Nov–late Dec); also open between daily between Christmas and New Year

Warwick: Warwick Castle – Warwick, CV34 4QU www.warwick-castle.com Tel 0870 442 2000 Open all year, daily 10am–6pm (to 5pm in Oct–Mar)

Warwick: Lord Leycester Hospital – High Street, Warwick, CV34 4BH www.lordleycester.com Tel 01926 491422 Open all year, Tue–Sun & BH Mon 10am–5pm (to 4pm in winter)

Winkburn Hall – Winkburn, Newark, Nottinghamshire, NG22 8PQ Tel 01636 636465 Open by appointment

Woolsthorpe Manor – Water Lane, Woolsthorpe-by-Colsterworth, Grantham, Lincolnshire, NG33 5PD www.nationaltrust.org.uk Tel 01476 860338 Open early Mar–late Oct, Wed–Sun (Sat–Sun in early–late Mar & early–late Oct) 1–5pm (from 11am on Sat–Sun in Jul–Aug)

Worksop: Mr Straw's House – 7 Blyth Grove, Worksop, Nottinghamshire, S81 0JG www.nationaltrust.org.uk Tel 01909 482380 Open mid-Mar–early Nov, Tue–Sat 11am–5pm

Index

Main entries for houses are in **bold**

Discover Britain's Historic Houses: The Midlands

Reader's Digest Project Team
Series editor Christine Noble
Art editor Jane McKenna
Picture researcher Christine Hinze
Caption writer/copy editor Caroline Smith
Proofreader Ron Pankhurst
Indexer Marie Lorimer
Product production manager Claudette Bramble
Production controller Katherine Bunn

Reader's Digest General Books
Editorial director Julian Browne
Art director Anne-Marie Bulat
Managing editor Nina Hathway
Picture resource manager Sarah Stewart-Richardson
Pre-press account manager Dean Russell

Colour origination Colour Systems Limited, London
Printed and bound in Europe by Arvato, Iberia

We are committed to both the quality of our products and the service we provide to our customers. We value your comments, so please feel free to contact us on **08705 113366** or via our web site at **www.readersdigest.co.uk**

If you have any comments or suggestions about the content of our books, you can contact us at: **gbeditorial@readersdigest.co.uk**

Published by The Reader's Digest Association Limited, 11 Westferry Circus, Canary Wharf, London E14 4HE

This book was designed, edited and produced by The Reader's Digest Association Limited based on material from *England's Thousand Best Houses* by Simon Jenkins, first published by Allen Lane, the Penguin Press, a publishing division of Penguin Books Ltd.

Copyright © Simon Jenkins 2003

Concept code UK0149/L/S
Book code 634-012 UP0000-1
ISBN 978 0 276 44407 4
Oracle code 356600012H.00.24